The American History Series

SERIES EDITORS

John Hope Franklin, *Duke University*
A. S. Eisenstadt, *Brooklyn College*

Carl Ubbelohde
CASE WESTERN RESERVE UNIVERSITY

The American Colonies and the British Empire

1607–1763

SECOND EDITION

HARLAN DAVIDSON, INC.
WHEELING, ILLINOIS 60090-6000

Copyright © 1968, 1975
Harlan Davidson, Inc.

Library of Congress Cataloging in Publication Data

Ubbelohde, Carl.
   The American colonies and the British Empire, 1607–1763.

   (The American history series.)
   Includes bibliographical references and index.
   1. United States—Politics and government—Colonial period,
ca. 1600–1775.   2. Great Britain—Colonies—America—
Administration.   I. Title.
E188.U2   1975   320.9'73'02   75-17525
ISBN 0-88295-767-8

Cover design: Roger Eggers
Cover illustration: Historical Pictures Service, Chicago.

Manufactured in the United States of America
97 7 MG

For Susan, Nell, Libby, and Kate

EDITORS' FOREWORD

Every generation writes its own history, for the reason that it sees the past in the foreshortened perspective of its own experience. This has certainly been true of the writing of American history. The practical aim of our historiography is to offer us a more certain sense of where we are going by helping us understand the road we took in getting where we are. If the substance and nature of our historical writing is changing, it is precisely because our own generation is redefining its direction, much as the generations that preceded us redefined theirs. We are seeking a newer direction, because we are facing new problems, changing our values and premises, and shaping new institutions to meet new needs. Thus, the vitality of the present inspires the vitality of our writing about our past. Today's scholars are hard at work reconsidering every major field of our history: its politics, diplomacy, economy, society, mores, values, sexuality, and status, ethnic, and race relations. No less significantly, our scholars are using newer modes of investigation to probe the ever-expanding domain of the American past.

Our aim, in this American History Series, is to offer the reader a survey of what scholars are saying about the central themes and issues of American history. To present these themes and issues, we have invited scholars who have made notable contributions to the respective fields in which they are writing. Each volume offers the reader a sufficient factual and narrative account for perceiving the larger dimensions of its particular subject. Addressing their respective themes, our authors have undertaken, moreover, to present the conclusions derived by the principal writers on these themes. Beyond that, the authors present their own conclusions about those aspects of their respective subjects that have been matters of difference and controversy. In effect, they have written not only about where the subject stands in today's historiography but also about where they stand on their subject. Each volume closes with an extensive critical essay on the writings of the major authorities on its particular theme.

The books in this series are designed for use in both basic and advanced courses in American history. Such a series has a particular utility in times such as these, when the traditional format of our American history courses is being altered to accommodate a greater diversity of texts and reading materials. The series offers a number of distinct advantages. It extends and deepens the dimensions of course work in American history. In proceeding beyond the confines of the traditional textbook, it makes clear that the study of our past is, more than the student might otherwise infer, at once complex, sophisticated, and profound. It presents American history as a subject of continuing vitality and fresh investigation. The work of experts in their respective fields, it opens up to the student the rich findings of historical inquiry. It invites the student to join, in major fields of research, the many groups of scholars who are pondering anew the central themes and problems of our past. It challenges the student to participate actively in exploring American history and to collaborate in the creative and rigorous adventure of seeking out its wider reaches.

John Hope Franklin

Abraham S. Eisenstadt

CONTENTS

ONE

Building an Empire

There were American colonies, established by English people, before there was a British Empire. After a series of ill-fated attempts to sustain an English settlement in the Western Hemisphere during the sixteenth century, the tiny group of settlers dispatched by the Virginia Company to the shores of the Chesapeake achieved historic distinction as the planters of the first permanent English colony in the New World. The year was 1607. In the course of the next four decades, other Englishmen migrated to American shores for a variety of reasons. By the middle of the century, transplanted Englishmen were grouped in a cluster of communities in New England; Virginia had been joined in the Chesapeake area by the Calvert proprietary province of Maryland; Englishmen had developed plantations on islands in the Caribbean. But there was, as of 1650, no empire, for these colonies had been conceived, born, and were struggling with their childhood problems without general supervision from the homeland and without official blueprints charting their future destinies.

The British Empire came into being in the second half of the seventeenth century. It was born during the years of the Interregnum, while the Stuart family was temporarily driven from the throne of England. Nurtured during the era called the Restoration, the empire reached maturity during the closing years of the century. It began as an economic concept, erected upon the core idea of tying the trade lanes of the miscellaneous English overseas possessions into a mercantile network for sustaining national strength. But economic regulation almost inevitably brought increased awareness of, and interest in, political and constitutional relationships. Ideas of uniformity and consolidation of control soon became imperial goals. The drive for conformity reflected additional interests after England and her colonies embarked on a series of military struggles against France, and later Spain as well, along with their New World empires.

By the early years of the eighteenth century, the basic structure of the first British Empire (of which the mainland American colonies were only one part) had been shaped. The patterns which had evolved would remain largely unmodified during the next six decades. Of course, from time to time minor alterations were needed to satisfy specific interests or elements on one or both sides of the ocean. Sometimes the configurations were slightly shifted to accommodate newer developments. But generally, imperfect and disarranged though the patterns might have appeared then and sometimes appear now, it was not until after 1763 that major (and in the eyes of Americans, unconstitutional) changes precipitated the crisis of the American Revolution.

The voluminous details contained in the extant records of the first century and a half of European life in the American wilderness, including at times distressingly contradictory evidence concerning motivations and beliefs, tend to obscure the outlines of the pattern of imperial relationships. Historians have not always agreed upon the shape or dimensions of the pattern; they have often disagreed even more sharply on their relative consequences. Some scholars are inclined to argue that the very concept of empire exists more fully in the minds and imaginations of present-day historians, attempting to find orderly systems in past ages, than it ever did in the minds of Englishmen or Americans in the seventeenth and eighteenth centuries. What makes the problem of assessing the history of the American colonies doubly difficult is the fact that, in time, the colonies ceased to be colonies. Having established themselves as independent states and having joined together to fashion a republican federation, the revolutionary generation justified, in part, its actions on the benefits to come from separation from the empire.

Naturally, then, the men of the young republic who wrote the earliest histories of the colonial experience to create a heritage and tradition for their new nation emphasized the local, colonial part of the empire. The virtues of pilgrims seeking religious freedoms on the shores of the new continent, the values of democratically contrived town meetings and representative assemblies—these were the staples of the earliest American colonial history. The British Empire, with its restrictions and regulations stifling freedoms and opportunities for settlers, was a horrible handicap, a formidable hurdle the brave American pioneers encountered along the road to freedom. George Bancroft used several volumes of his *History of the United States of America* (1834–1874) to explain the problem. The American colonists had been virtuous; the British full of vice, for in Europe "it was a period of corruption. . . . It would have been very easy for the British government to have conciliated affection and respect . . . but the avidity of the persons holding office was constant and too strong." Especially at fault was the "mercantilist restrictive system . . . the superstition of that age. Capitalists worshipped it; statesmen were overawed by it; philosophers dared not question it." "All questions on colonial liberty and affairs were decided from the point of view of English commerce and the interests of the great landholders." But "the system of trade and navigation, being founded in selfish injustice, was doomed . . . to expire," for "popular liberty had thriven vigorously" in the colonies, "like the tree by the rivers of water, that grows in the night-time. . . ."

Such history was American colonial history, not British imperial history. It was written by Americans, for Americans. It satisfied the people of a relatively isolated, emerging nation who believed in their unique destiny and desired an historical narrative to provide a heritage consistent with that destiny. For a hundred years after the creation of the United States as a sovereign nation, its history of its origins was cast in such forms.

The last years of the nineteenth century and the opening decades of the twentieth brought a change. The older history might satisfy the amateur historian; it might have its uses in grammar-school textbooks and Fourth of July celebrations. But there had now come into prominence historical scholars who held an ideal of objectively reporting past events that led them to fear interjection of personal or national prejudices into their history. Modeled after the "scientific" historians of Germany, trained in the seminars of the new graduate schools, working with tools of unmatched caliber, and dedicated to a depth of scholarship previously unknown, they embarked upon a quest that radically altered the contours of American colonial history.

These historians argued for a fresh start in the study of America's origins. They spoke for a colonial history that was unimpassioned by patriotic prejudice and anti-British inclinations, or viewed only through the window of the American Revolution. Scholars such as Herbert L. Osgood, Charles M. Andrews, George L. Beer, and their disciples studied the first British Empire, particularly as it developed and matured in relation to the mainland American colonies. They avidly sought out and recorded the history of the agencies of empire; they analyzed theories of imperial control; they came to a sympathetic understanding of the difficulties of imperial administration. As they studied and wrote, they tended to forget the American scene, devoting more and more attention to the details of statesmanship and placemanship, commissions and bureaucracy in London. They were not unaware of their self-imposed limitations. Charles M. Andrews, in the preface to the fourth volume of *The Colonial Period of American History* (1934–1937), defined anew the boundaries of his concern: "Whether the colonial and commercial policies of the seventeenth- and eighteenth-century statesmen and capitalists were politically or economically sound or unsound is not the question; nor is it necessary at this point to determine the effects of these policies upon the colonists themselves or to compare them with present-day ideas. All I am attempting to do . . . is to make clear as best I may the essential features of these policies as England shaped them and to trace their history from the beginning of England's experience with colonies down to the eve of the American Revolution." And, a little later on, ". . . the subject forms an integral part of that most fundamental of colonial questions, the relationship which existed for more than one hundred and fifty years between England and her colonies overseas."

Of course, no two scholars of this "imperial" group followed exactly the same definition. Yet common to all was their conviction that the fundamental question as stated by Andrews—"the relationship . . . between England and her colonies overseas"—was exactly the right question. To answer it historians needed to know precisely what the empire looked like, especially from its center in London. This emphasis left less and less energy to direct toward studies of the response of the colonists in America to imperial policies or to the indigenous development of social, economic, political—or any other—patterns within the colonies themselves. Despite this drift away from native shores, these scholars contributed a magnificent historical literature. They taught an understanding of the structure and problems of empire, breaking the older mold of colonial history which had seen significance only in terms of the American scene, substituting in its place a fuller, more realistic accounting of the colonies *as colonies* within a far-flung empire. And, to a large extent, they liked what they saw. Viewing the empire from London led them to a sympathetic understanding of Britain's imperial problems as well as general satisfaction with the policies and agencies Britain devised to deal with those problems.

But the age of the "imperialists" seemed to pass. Enchantment with their viewpoint and emphasis declined from its ready acceptance in the early decades of the twentieth century. There are many reasons why American colonial history, cast in the framework of British imperial history, should have become less satisfying than it was in the first half of the century. For the American of 1900, there might be exhilaration in the very idea of "empire" when empires, including a new American empire, were current political issues. To the citizen of the United States in 1917, a sympathetic study of British imperial problems in the eighteenth century might appear illuminating as he searched for Anglo-American understanding in a war-torn world. But increasingly, as economic and social and intellectual history turned aside older emphases on political and constitutional problems, historians began to desert the "imperial" stance and to return in their studies to the American scene.

Part of the reaction can be traced directly to the increasing emphasis on economic forces as determinants in human activities. The quarter century from 1920 to 1945 saw the publication of studies that concentrated on economic motivations and economic effects instead of the institutions and policies Andrews had marked off as his field of interest. Andrews might be uninterested in the "soundness" of Britain's commercial policies or in their effect on the colonies, but Louis Hacker, Curtis Nettels, and a new generation were not. Hacker's studies encompassed the question of imperial relations as part of his writing on American capitalism, but his interpretation of the colonies' role in the British Empire emphasized the restrictive nature of the imperial connection. The questions Andrews put aside Hacker took up, and his answers described the economic effects of the empire in dichotomous terms, with American merchant capitalism smothered by the mother country's restrictive policies, designed to favor British capitalists at the expense of the Americans. Curtis Nettels also sought to understand the effect of imperial regulation in terms of economic results and from them the attitudes of the people affected. The picture Nettels drew is not the portrait of collision between two aspiring capitalistic groups of Hacker's work; it is rather a mosaic of varied hues, with restrictions of serious consequences at some points, failures in policies at others, and colonial benefits at still others.

Hacker and Nettels were only two of many who found the "imperialist" version of history unsatisfactory. The disenchantment they represented was to be followed after 1945 by a further turn in interests and emphases. By then the cycle was almost complete. Thereafter the British Empire no longer seemed a satisfactory focus of investigation for many colonial historians. Increasingly in the years of the Cold War and its warmer moments, when the "American Way of Life" seemed threatened, American scholars searched for national origins within the local scene. They recorded their findings in monographs of generally limited scope, often contenting themselves with biographies of colonial merchants, political leaders, molders of American thought. Or, if surveying instruments of political or economic regulation, they centered their emphasis in the colonies, rather than in imperial agencies.

Yet like all good history, the story of the American colonies in the British Empire continues to be a layered creation. No serious scholar ignores the findings, or cavalierly dismisses the interpretations, of the earlier "imperialists" or their successors such as Lawrence H. Gipson or Leonard W. Labaree. Although the emphasis has changed, the best colonial history still is written with an awareness of the problem of defining the place of the colonies in the empire and with a curiosity to understand and assess the consequences of the imperial relationship for the Americans who lived in the seventeenth and eighteenth centuries.

One of the most obvious differences separating the "imperialists" and the newer "nationalists" (if they can be so termed) rises out of the separate ways in which the two groups viewed the nature of the British Empire. The "imperialists" generally assumed or believed that the imperial machinery Britain created to supervise the empire worked quite well. Britain and her colonies both benefited from the imperial relationship; imperial theories and the empire in practice were basically one and the same. The more recent studies of American colonial origins, focused more closely on the colonial scene, have emphasized evidence which suggests the opposite. The newer scholars have been impressed with the significance of the departure of the American colonists from the theoretical empire, developing local controls and procedures which shifted actual power from the parent state to the colonies. In this view there were two empires: the empire of theory and the empire of reality. The first, and the one that the "imperialists" emphasized, was a relatively static enterprise. The other, the actual empire, was constantly subjected to stresses and strains, and, as conceived by the American colonists at the close of the colonial era, was a very different entity from the theoretical empire.

This difference in viewpoint is by no means the only problem of interpretation faced by students of America's early years. The pages that follow will indicate some of the other areas of disagreement among the expert craftsmen of history. This book attempts to describe historians' understandings of the formal apparatus of empire, as well as the economic and political interrelationships between Britain and the American mainland provinces. There were, of course, many other trans-Atlantic ties—cultural, scientific, religious, artistic—that altered, enhanced, diminished, the political and economic threads that bound together the "homeland" in Europe and the overseas dominions. To start at the beginning, we will briefly recount the story of how the English empire was created.

MOTIVATIONS AND ASSUMPTIONS

Those English people responsible for the creation of the first British Empire were motivated by three basic considerations. Englishmen worked at empire building in the New World and strove to maintain that empire for economic, strategic, and social reasons. These are broad classifications. Within any one of them may be found a remarkable variety of expressions of interest and intent. Yet they are reasonably satisfactory labels for discussing motivations for creation of the first British Empire.

Economically, England turned to her American possessions

as an important element in increasing her national strength. This attention to empire may be seen in both the private and the public economic sectors in England. As trade with America developed during the seventeenth century, private entrepreneurs sought to expand their sources of profit, looking to the English state for such help as could be given. At the same time, the colonies provided royal revenues of considerable significance to the ruling Stuart kings, thereby enhancing the national goal of building an independent, self-sufficient state. Within these broad objectives, private and public interests coincided and found expression in the relatively ill-defined, but nonetheless persuasive, theories known as "mercantilism."

Both private economic interests and state planners believed that colonies would be useful to the mother country as sources of raw materials, as producers of noncompetitive strategic goods unavailable in the homeland, and as markets for fabricated products. The overseas dominions were to be perpetual dependencies which would and should always contribute to the accumulation of wealth in the parent state. All this would ensure the rising power of the English nation in the new age of costly warfare.

This economic impulse was the first major cause for the creation of the empire; it remained a guiding motivation throughout the history of that first empire. But, in time, other arguments attracted adherents and brought additional emphasis to empire building. Toward the close of the seventeenth century, England entered the long series of wars with France which would lead ultimately to the impressive British triumphs in the Great War for Empire, ending in 1763. During this Anglo-French rivalry, the American provinces of both contestants became increasingly significant in strategic planning. Englishmen who had long thought of the American outposts merely as economic dependencies changed their views to consider the colonies as strategic entities, vulnerable to attack by enemy forces but also useful as bases for operations against those same foes. Thus theoretical strategic advantages of American colonies, set forth much earlier by men like Richard Hakluyt, who had identified the potential benefit of colonies in providing opportunities by which England could strike against her then enemy, Spain, became realities in the eighteenth century.

In addition to economic impulses and strategic considerations, the outposts of empire in the New World were also useful instruments for effecting social change. The colonies could be, and were, havens for oppressed people and conveniently distant dumping grounds for misfits and dissidents—the religiously unorthodox, the economically unemployed, the criminally convicted—all the potentially dangerous segments of the English population. The colonies could be, and were, useful as laboratories for social, sometimes even utopian, experimentation. The colonies could have been, but never fully became, the scene of religious endeavors, especially the conversion of the native "heathen" to Protestant Christianity.

No carefully charted blueprint ever was drawn and adhered to, neatly balancing these various objectives. England never created a "yardstick" for precisely measuring imperial affairs against a set of established standards. In fact, imperial theories sometimes collided with each other, making choices among alternative actions difficult to determine. Equal emphasis was never placed on all objectives of the empire at any one time or by all groups of people. Since the first British Empire lasted for more than one hundred years, shifts in objectives and policies were to be expected. But a few relatively constant assumptions remained basic in imperial thought throughout the era.

First was the assumption, altered in only a very few minor instances late in the era, that colony building was to be a private endeavor. The Crown was willing to donate, on its own terms, the real estate involved, and from time to time to grant concessions to encourage the initial development of colonies. For example, in some cases commercial regulations were suspended for a limited number of years. But, except for that, private resources were to be employed. The adventurers and businessmen of the time had to accumulate the courage and the money to plant the outposts across the seas. No royal funds could be used to promote the great goal of colony building.

Second, once established, the colonies were to remain perpetually in an inferior or subsidiary position to the parent state. For administrative convenience or for encouragement of particular purposes, the colonists might be allowed measures of limited local control, but, although unevenly applied, the universal assumption held in England was that the provinces were not, and as far as the future was concerned, never would be, equals with the mother country. There was no provision for eventually adopting mature colonies into organic union with the parent state. England would remain the center, the colonies dependencies.

Finally, a third assumption was developed concerning diplomacy and defense. While local protection, mostly against hostile Indians, remained a colonial concern, as the collisions between England and France spread into the empires, it became understood that England owed some obligation for providing security to her "wards" across the ocean. Varying greatly from time to time and place to place, by the end of the era the colonists and Britain both assumed that the major burden of defense would fall on the mother country, although some elements of a partnership in war were always expected and the colonists were called upon to contribute to the planning, leadership, manpower, and financing of imperial defense and expansion. Similarly, although "neighborhood" agreements were sometimes arranged, as, for example, between New England and New Netherlands, in establishing a temporary dividing line, diplomacy, like defense, was a matter for imperial rather than colonial determination.

While these assumptions—private rather than public investment in colonial enterprises, perpetual dependency, and imperial control of diplomacy and, eventually, defense—remained more or less permanent bases of imperial thought and action, the motivations for building and maintaining the empire—economic, strategic, social—were constantly being tested by environment and situation in the New World. Empires are not, by their very nature, unilateral operations. No matter how cleverly conceived English policy might be in terms of furthering national interests at home, realities in America might make alterations necessary. So long as the imperial statesmen provided room in their plans for adjustments to the realities of colonial life, their policies stood good chance of success. But often, given the distances involved, the slowness of communication, the natural tendencies for Englishmen to think in terms of the homeland and American colonists to think in terms of their own welfare, American realities modified and at times completely frustrated the "best laid plans" of England.

How far American realities had moved from English theories was not completely apparent until after 1763, and then it was obvious that the same ideas of empire no longer satisfied parent and child. However, until that time, the assumptions seemed reasonably workable, and for the better part of the century, with adjustments and modifications smoothing out the rougher edges, the relationship between homeland and colonies continued to provide a framework within which both experienced increasing prosperity, making Britain and her empire the growing envy of much of Western Europe.

THE EARLY PLANTINGS

It is often asserted that England established her first empire in a fit of absentmindedness. Or, stated another way, in the middle years of the seventeenth century, England seemed to "discover" her colonies in the New World and began to consider those colonies in a changed way. Formerly, if thought of at all, they were viewed as isolated, individual outposts on the edge of the vast continent of North America, variously conceived and maintained, but in no sense forming a major economic, and certainly not a strategic, unit of national strength. Then, in the days of the English Civil War and the years of the Restoration that followed, those formerly almost forgotten outposts emerged as properties potentially valuable to the realm, capable of developing into economic assets and worthy of consideration as future sources of national strength.

Considering that in the years between Jamestown's founding in 1607 and the beginnings of the English Civil War in 1641 more than 70,000 Englishmen left their homeland for various parts of America, it is obvious that most Englishmen knew something about the colonies in the New World. Too much effort had been expended, too many pounds sterling had been risked, too many lottery tickets had been purchased and missionary funds donated for there to have been no knowledge of the overseas activities. But what was true, and remained so during most of the first British Empire, was that affairs at home and in the more familiar world of continental Europe crowded the mind. This priority of domestic and European concern was to continue throughout the seventeenth and eighteenth centuries. Under the circumstances, only a very few men and women were immediately and directly involved in overseas colonization. For that reason, and perhaps also because of the great variety of circumstances out of which the colonies had come into existence, decades passed before many Englishmen began to perceive overall patterns in, and possibilities of common benefits from, the ill-assorted outposts in America.

By the time such considerations led to action, and the empire was created, there existed in America a strange miscellany of adolescent colonies. These were grouped geographically in three regions: the Chesapeake area, where Virginians, the first colonists, and settlers in Maryland, the fief of the Calverts, were engaged in developing their tobacco society; the New England area, with Massachusetts Bay as the hub, and the satellites in Plymouth, New Haven, Connecticut, Rhode Island, along with outposts in New Hampshire and Maine; and, finally, in the Caribbean, the island possessions including St. Christopher, Antigua, Nevis, Montserrat, Barbados, and Bermuda.

Some of these colonies came into being as offshoots of trading companies chartered by the Crown. The constitutional theory undergirding them was relatively uncomplicated. Overseas lands claimed by England (fundamentally on John Cabot's official exploratory voyage of 1497) were the Crown's to dispose of as it saw fit. Venturesome merchants, anticipating profits from commerce, petitioned for royal permission to form chartered companies to engage in trade, exploration, and colonization. The technique had been used for a half century to organize commercial enterprises in other parts of the world before it was applied to the trading company charter granted in 1606 by James I to the Virginia Company. The trading company charter also was used for the Massachusetts experiment in 1629. The Massachusetts charter remained intact, but the Virginia Company had been dissolved in 1624, and its colony had come under direct royal control.

A second type of royal grant had resulted in a differently structured group of colonies. The Crown had seen fit to bestow upon individuals or groups proprietary privileges to certain parts of the American continent. Caribbean islands, Maryland, and, by subgrants, certain parts of New England, had been disposed of in this way and still were connected legally to the homeland (that is, to the Crown) through the thread of proprietary patents.

Finally, there were indigenously created covenant-type settlements, which legally and constitutionally had no royal sanction at all, but rather were the result of settlers taking matters of government and internal organization into their own hands, forming their own political structures. Connecticut and the Rhode Island communities had come into being in this fashion.

Thus England's American outposts, as of 1650, shared no single type of legal tie with the mother country. In the untidy mixture could be found four distinct styles of colonial structures: royal provinces, trading company endeavors, proprietary colonies, and covenant communities. In time this circumstance would engage the talents and imaginations of men dedicated to reducing the colonies to a common pattern.

The untidiness of the constitutional relationships between the American colonies and England was matched, or surpassed, by the variety of impulses responsible for the creation and initial settlement of the outposts. In no case was the settlement of any colony the result of a single, exclusive motive. While economic gain might appear the most significant force motivating the members of the Virginia Company, a variety of other impulses generated some of their aspirations—religiously inspired dreams of converting the "heathen" natives; patriotism in crowding close to and contesting with Spain her New World empire; adventuresomeness which needed outlet and found it in the strange new lands across the western seas. In the same way, to picture early Massachusetts Bay as an exclusively religious enterprise, and fail to consider the social and economic aspirations of its founders, creates a distorted portrait.

And if common patterns did not exist for the constitutional relationships between the American colonies and the homeland, or in the motivations that had brought them into being, the same is true, and even amplified, in the colonies' development after their initial settlement. Many elements and ingredients combined to produce varied results—geography, climate, intent of sponsors, natural resources, types of colonists attracted to the settlement. Yet even here some classification is possible. In New England, self-sustaining agriculture, with other emphases on fish and timber for export, along with increasing interest in general commercial activities, became the pattern of life. The Chesapeake area, after false starts in gold seeking and silk culture, had, by midcentury, adopted a tobacco economy, although it then lacked the elements of huge plantations and the predominantly black slave labor force that would characterize it later. The Caribbean islands turned as naturally to the sugar products they could grow so profitably and which, in English eyes, were blessed because they did not compete with home production.

Thus not in constitutional structure, nor founders' purposes, nor economic development did England's American settlements share common patterns. Generally isolated from each other by huge stretches of forest or salt water, the colonies during their first decades amounted to little more than struggling beachheads, precariously poised on the edge of the American coastline. Of course these New World Englishmen did not have the continent all to themselves. They shared it with the natives, and with Europeans from Spain and France, Holland and Sweden. The Spanish were the most feared and the most envied, for they seemed to have found the richest parts of the New World and had grown powerful from the fortunes they had shipped back to Spain. Yet English fears were evaporating. The fact that island properties in the West Indies, so close to New Spain, could be colonized was impressive in itself, and soon new plans were afoot to contest even further the Spanish hold on the Caribbean. The French, like the English, were only beginning to reap success from their colonizing ventures, centered in the St.

Lawrence Valley. Contacts between Englishmen and Frenchmen in the New World in the first half of the century primarily were limited to the fishing areas off the Newfoundland shores. The Dutch, who soon had reduced the Swedish enterprises on the Delaware River, were somewhat more obviously in the way, for their holdings in the area of future New York not only geographically separated the New England and Chesapeake settlements, but also offered the Dutch merchants a base of operations from which to trade within the English colonies.

In time direct contests with these neighbors would take place, but for the immediate moment there were other events to consider. In fact, as of 1641 a curtain descended even on new colonizing activities in English America. For the next two decades, the homeland was torn internally by civil war, the destruction of royal rule, the execution of Charles I, the institution of Parliamentary rule, the Protectorate of Oliver Cromwell, and finally the return to the monarchy, with the restoration of Charles II. In such times there could be little inclination and less energy for new colonizing activities in America.

STEPS TOWARD EMPIRE

Despite the lull in initiating new colonial ventures, however, the twenty years from 1640 to 1660, in many ways, were as significant an era for the future British Empire in America as any other twenty-year period until the time of the American Revolution, more than a century later. The contest in England between Crown and Parliamentary forces, culminating in the demise of royal rule, brought two major considerations concerning America to the attention of policymakers. First, the elimination of royal control brought into question the constitutional bases upon which the American colonies were founded. And commercial rivalries with other European nations caused some Englishmen to look upon the overseas outposts as something more than separate, isolated communities, viewing them instead as units of a potentially integrated, expanded "empire" beyond the seas.

The first of these new considerations arose from the developments within revolutionary England. When Parliament replaced the Crown as the supreme power in England, what, if any, alterations were required in the constitutional relationships with the overseas colonies? Those colonies, so far as they were bound to England, were bound to the Crown: Virginia under direct royal control; Massachusetts, Maryland, and the West Indian possessions by royal charters. As Parliament assumed authority at home, Crown rights and powers became Parliament's, including control of the American dominions. But events in some parts of the New World soon demonstrated that some of the colonists thought differently.

The New England settlements, it was believed, would cause no great amount of trouble. Puritan themselves, they were expected to look with favor upon events in England. Ironically, it is true, the leading New England colony, Massachusetts Bay, assumed a bold posture as an independent republican community, developing even more highly its uniquely separate and independent theories of localism. The Chesapeake and West Indian provinces, however, were a different matter. In Virginia both the legislature and the royal governor, William Berkeley, had denied the legitimacy of the revolutionary English government, insisting on continuing their allegiance and devotion to the deposed Stuart family. In Maryland, where the proprietor's fellow Catholics had been struggling against Puritan settlers for some time, a similar declaration of allegiance to the Stuart cause issued from the proprietor's governor.

Retraction of such statements of disobedience to the new regime was required, and in 1650 Parliament enacted a coercive statute, dispelling all doubts about its intention to establish supremacy over the colonies. The act set forth a licensing system for all foreign vessels trading with America as well as a temporary commercial prohibition against the wayward provinces of Maryland, Virginia, and those Caribbean islands that had also proclaimed loyalty to Charles. In time a Parliamentary commission arrived in the New World to receive the submission of the provinces to the Commonwealth government. Once reduced to acknowledgment of Parliamentary supremacy, the colonies were constitutionally "established" in a fashion acceptable to the English authorities.

More significant (in terms of later development of the empire) than this tidying up of constitutional relationships was the new way the Puritan regime in England viewed the American colonies as part of a larger, total unit—something like a young empire. Reflections of this different concept of overseas enterprises are apparent in the "Western Design" of Oliver Cromwell, an ambitious blueprint for direct contest with Spain in the New World. Before the Cromwellian era had run its course, the "Design" would bring conquest of Jamaica and inclusion of that island in the orbit of English control.

And even more portentous as a reflection of "imperial" thought was Parliament's enactment of the first comprehensive commercial legislation regarding the New World colonies. The Navigation Act of 1651 implemented the principles of the coercive legislation of the previous year and carried even further the commercial regulation laid down by that statute. Designed to bring ultimate superiority to England's mercantile operations within the English "empire," the Act of 1651 set forth a basic prohibition closing the trade of the colonies to all except shippers from England or other English colonies.

This was neither the first commercial regulation regarding the colonies, nor was it the first time that Parliament, as an agency, had legislated regarding overseas possessions. Earlier the tobacco trade had been regulated, and imports into England from the Chesapeake plantations had been given a favored position in the kingdom, including a prohibition against tobacco culture at home. At the same time, tobacco from America had been subjected to importation duties of some significance to the royal treasury. Also Parliament, at earlier times, legislated against foreign trade with the American dominions, but that legislation had gone largely ignored and unenforced.

The new statute in 1651, however, because of its comprehensive nature and its objectives, signaled the beginnings of a new era of regulation, to last for one hundred years, each enactment more closely defining the commercial and industrial roles allowed the American colonies. Thus the act stands as one of the more significant milestones along the road leading to the creation of an empire. And the legislation, largely economic in motivation, gives indication that, at the beginning, the creation of the empire was very much an economic consideration.

This Parliamentary measure of 1651 has been of more than ordinary interest to historians searching for the origins of the first British Empire. They have not always agreed about the specific conditions of 1651 resulting in the enactment of the general policies. It seems clear from what has been written about the act's antecedents that it marked no sudden departure from previous attempts at commercial regulation, attempts extending backward in time through centuries of English trade, and through decades as far as such measures touched colonial commerce. And it also indicates the generally accepted English mercantilist view of national interest, which was by no means a startling innovation in the English thought of 1651.

Even so, granting the antecedents and earlier general acceptance of the basic purposes of the act, Charles M. Andrews's explanation appears to retain validity. In *The Colonial Period of American History*, Andrews asserted that the immediate cause of the Parliamentary enactment of 1651 was the growing success of Dutch merchants in carrying away the exports of England's Caribbean and Chesapeake possessions. Commercial rivalry with the Dutch, if it was eventually to end in English superiority, needed to be defined in such a way that England's colonies did not contribute to Dutch strength. Since the Dutch had been particularly successful in their competition with the English in the American trade, the exclusion of all foreigners from the dominions, if properly enforced, would rid the English merchants trading with America of that competition, build England's mercantile strength generally, and in so doing advance the overall national strength as well.

Thus, by 1660, England had experienced the initial stirrings toward empire. The supreme authority from "home" had quieted restless disloyalty to its regime; a flurry of interest had been generated toward an expansion of overseas activities; and, most significant of all, the rudiments of a system of commercial regulation had been legislated. Out of the turmoil of revolutionary England had come the first tokens of a new entity—an English empire in the New World.

THE RESTORATION EMPIRE

In 1660 Puritan government in England ended; the Stuart family was restored to the throne. The next three decades would see relatively consistent efforts to construct an orderly, logically arranged empire in America, although the motivation was not completely new. What had been begun during the Interregnum would be continued and expanded, for the regulation of overseas commerce for the benefit of the homeland proved as pleasant and desirable to the forces ruling post-Restoration England as it had been to the merchant groups sponsoring the policies during Parliament's supremacy. Charles II's return to England brought involvement from a greater variety of interest groups, groups that are described by Michael Kammen in *Empire and Interest: The American Colonies and the Politics of Mercantilism* (1970). These interest groups—the chartered companies, industrial groups, religious sects, towns (London, Bristol), land companies, the Irish interest, the landed interest, the labor interest, the "moneyed" interest—competed for favors from the state in a fashion that might have subverted the national interest; indeed, as Kammen explains: "although mercantilist doctrine stressed the importance of national economic interests, it also contained implicitly the potential disharmony between particular commercial groups, individual merchants, and classes on the one hand, and the welfare of the commonwealth as a whole, on the other."

Yet despite the jostling among the interest groups, and the potential for competition between special interests and the nation, most advocates looked toward continued, or increased, imperial regulation as beneficial. As English merchants continued to press for protection against Dutch and other foreign competitors in the American trade, other economic interests sought extension of regulatory enactments to protect or expand their endeavors. The Crown itself was vitally concerned with such regulation, for it would gain revenues from effective imperial control of colonial commerce. And, as regulation was extended and the need to administer policies more effectively was realized, there grew up in the department and commission offices a group of imperially minded servants of the state, a more or less permanent group of men, some high-ranking lords, others civil service placemen, committed to the concept of building an English empire. To further the welfare and interests of the state, these men perceived it their duty to define and regulate more precisely the overseas colonies, believing this could be most easily effected by furthering unity among and control over the American dominions.

As the empire builders turned to their tasks in the quarter century following the Restoration, they had more components available for restructuring than had been in existence in 1660. In rapid order the already established settlements in America were joined by new colonies. By the early 1680s four new colonial entities had been created. Between the Delaware River and the New England settlements, where the Dutch had operated commercial ventures from their American outpost, the English, after conquest of the Dutch settlements, shaped their acquisition into two proprietary enterprises—New York and New Jersey. Across the Delaware River, another proprietary province was begun by William Penn. And south of Virginia, in lands still claimed by Spain, Charles II carved out the proprietary grant called Carolina for a group of his friends and supporters.

While motivations for English expansion into New York and New Jersey, Pennsylvania, and Carolina were mixed, and the development of these new provinces varied greatly, common to all was the use of the proprietary patent as the constitutional basis for settlement. This consistency in form is indicative of the dominant political forces in Restoration England. No longer were trade and commerce the prime motives leading to overseas colonization; merchants and capitalists, by 1660, had come to understand that profits from initiating colonies could not be counted on while, conversely, the rewards from trade with already established colonies were of considerable potential. Nor was religious refuge any longer a major objective for most new colonial endeavors, although Pennsylvania provides an exception, and in no case can the religious motive be entirely discounted.

The basic impulse leading to these new proprietaries was the interest of the landed aristocratic class in England—men who, in the light of their own experience as landholders in England, looked upon English America primarily as a place to extend their landholding and their incomes. The use of the proprietary charter to gain increase in landed wealth, although utilizing a more antique form than the joint stock company charter, symbolizes the dominance of the landed English group in the formation of these new enterprises.

The form is not paradoxical in relation to the dominant group supporting the Restoration government at home, but it is ironic that, at the same time that Charles II severed large stretches of his American real estate from Crown control, handing over areas as perpetual proprietaries, other men in the kingdom, including close advisers to the king, were beginning to visualize the American colonies in more imperialistic terms which, if such plans were ever to succeed, demanded greater consolidation and control. Charles encouraged both groups at the same time, with one hand separating areas of North America from immediate royal control and with the other encouraging a policy of administering the dominions in a more efficient and perhaps a more economically rewarding way.

It should be noted, however, that while the Carolina and Duke of York grants of the 1660s tended, like the earlier Calvert patent, to place sweeping personal powers in the hands of the proprietors, by 1681 when Pennsylvania was granted to William Penn, the forces urging consolidation were able to exert rather significant restrictions upon that proprietor's powers. Among other clauses of Penn's charter reducing his authority and bringing Pennsylvania under closer royal control were the stipulations that laws of the province must be referred to the Privy Council for approval or disallowance; that the right of appeal to English courts must be open to settlers in the province; that an agent must be maintained in England to answer any charges of evasion of the navigation laws or other complaints; and that the local administration must cooperate with the customs officials established in the colony. These limitations on the proprietor's authority illustrate changes in imperial thought in the two decades since the Restoration.

The task of determining orderly arrangements between the older, existing colonies and the parent state was also an objective of the post-Restoration policymakers. The work to be done naturally differed from colony to colony because of the variety of previous arrangements that had been forged. In Virginia the task was relatively simple: restoration of Crown rule was implemented without difficulty in this oldest of the American dominions by merely returning the constitutional relationship to what it had been before the demise of royal control in England, even to the reestablishment of Sir William Berkeley to his former governorship. In the other Chesapeake colony, despite desires by some imperial planners to see Calvert's control extinguished, the province of Maryland (which had been restored to the proprietor in 1658) was continued in his control.

Patterns for reconstituting royal control in the West Indian areas were also rather clearly defined. Barbados, the Leeward Islands (St. Christopher, Nevis, Antigua, and Montserrat), and, at an even earlier date, the newly captured Spanish island of Jamaica were constituted royal provinces. In Barbados and the Leewards this meant reduction of a former proprietary; in Jamaica it meant transference from military rule to civilian control in royal form.

New England offered other situations. Rhode Island wanted to exchange the Parliamentary-based charter that Roger Williams had secured in 1644 for a royal acknowledgment of its existence; Connecticut sought the same security. Both colonies were fortunate, for despite later attempts by Charles II and his successor to reduce colonies to Crown control, in the first years of his rule Charles agreed to grant royal charters to the two colonies, accepting them as corporate entities and allowing them to continue their basically democratic governments. Thus Rhode Island, which had fought desperately to retain its identity against encroachments by its "orthodox" Puritan neighbors, and Connecticut, now also encompassing the New Haven colony within its borders, reached an early and, for themselves, very satisfactory solution to their problem of legitimating their independent status as nearly self-governing corporations.

Massachusetts Bay proved a different story. Her defiant attitude expressed during the Puritan regime in England, reflecting what Michael G. Hall in *The Glorious Revolution in America* (1964) has called the province's "de facto independence," could hardly be expected to abate with the return to power of the old enemy, the Stuart monarchy. Prosperous, powerful, and determined to retain local control of her destiny, the Bay Province was marked for special consideration by the post-Restoration empire builders. The "battle," however, proved a lengthy affair, and before its conclusion, England had moved a long way toward its goal of a consolidated empire in the New World.

During the first decade and a half following the Restoration, England not only continued but expanded the mercantile regulations begun by the Navigation Act of 1651 and, in addition, created more efficient methods for administering the commercial laws both in the colonies and at home. Since the Parliamentary Act of 1651 was of doubtful legality once Charles had been restored as king of England, some reenactment of the legislation was to be expected. Also to be considered was the fact that none of the American provinces had voluntarily complied with the act, most of the colonies having expressed outright hostility to the regulations. But rather than providing a mere restatement of that act, new legislation in 1660 (often termed the First Navigation Act) extended economic regulation to include a provision that certain significant staple products grown in the colonies, such as sugar, tobacco, and cotton, could be exported from the place of production only to England or to another English colony. Thus was begun the practice of listing or "enumerating" certain strategic commodities for shipment only within the empire or, if surpluses were not needed there, at least to be cleared from English ports in transshipment to other parts of the world, thereby insuring the carriage profits to English merchants and revenue proceeds to the Crown.

Next was added, in legislation of 1663 (the Staple Act), a formula for protecting the English merchant community interested in the American trade. This required that European goods destined for importation into the American colonies must be shipped via the homeland. A few commodities, including salt to New England, wine from the Azores and Madeira, and horses and servants from Ireland, were excepted. All else was subject to handling by English merchants, insuring them a monopoly in the source of manufactured goods brought to the colonies.

Ten years later a further Parliamentary enactment closed a loophole in the process of regulating enumerated goods. Merchants had presumably satisfied the earlier requirements by simply taking enumerated goods from the colonial port of origin to another colonial port and from there carrying the goods outside the empire, escaping customs payment. Now export duties, roughly equivalent to the English import duties, were required on enumerated products at the time they left the colonial port of origin. This enactment was particularly significant for future relations between England and her American colonies, since the duties required something more than haphazard enforcement by colonial governors. The need to provide orderly and efficient duty collections introduced customs officials into America. For the first time there now appeared in the English colonies a group of imperial officeholders specifically charged with enforcement of the trade laws.

While administrative posts were thus established in America, there was also created, in 1675, a new agency in England responsible for overseeing the imperial trade. After a variety of short-lived and generally less than satisfactory experiments with committees and commissions, the agency known as the Lords of Trade was created, charged with overall supervision of colonial affairs. A committee of Privy Councillors, the Lords of Trade developed its own administrative staff, through whose offices information about the colonies could be funneled and colonial affairs could be "cleared." Through its own appointed agents sent to America, the Lords of Trade could gather additional knowledge of colonial events upon which new policies for bringing order into imperial affairs could be built.

Thus, within the first fifteen years of restored Stuart rule, an expanded mercantile regulatory system, involving a more centralized agency than had been known before in England and entirely new officers on the American side of the Atlantic, had been established. While the plans were yet incomplete, and further efforts to consolidate the empire would be made later, by the mid-1670s empire building had progressed considerably.

REACTION IN AMERICA

The introduction of the new customs officers into the American colonies, necessitated by the Navigation Act of 1673, brought colonial theories and imperial regulations into a new focus for Americans. Flesh-and-blood Englishmen were now physically present in the colonies, charged with making the empire work as a day-to-day affair. Tied to these activities in America was the new agency, the Lords of Trade in England, directing colonial affairs in a more centralized fashion than had ever been attempted before.

This was not only a matter of laws enforced that perhaps had not been obeyed; this involved positions to be filled by men with a variety of motivations for their actions; it introduced both a cluster of individuals in positions of power in England espousing doctrines and concepts about the proper relationship between colonies and parent state and, even more potentially explosive, the arrival in America of Englishmen in a capacity never known before—agents of the new empire, interested in the colonies as sources of national strength *and* personal fortune, but often, unfortunately, unaware of the local circumstances affecting the Americans' attitudes toward the new regulations.

At one time historians were relatively content to trace the origins and development of the structure of regulation; to delineate the statutes of Parliament and the actions of the Lords of Trade and other English agencies that brought the rudiments of an empire into existence. But a further dimension has been added to our knowledge of the first British Empire—detailed analyses of the personalities involved in administering those regulations, which show, in addition to what the structure of empire was, the way in which it was actually put into operation. Michael G. Hall's study, *Edward Randolph and the American*

Colonies (1960), is especially useful in this context, for the author analyzes both Randolph's motivations and the colonists' reactions to him and his policies. Randolph was not only an advance agent of empire, making his way along the Atlantic coast of the American colonies as the authorized eyes and ears of the Lords of Trade; he was also an ambitious office seeker and fortune hunter, who looked upon the national interests of England and his own personal advancement as complementary, rather than competitive, objectives. He was, writes Bernard Bailyn in *The New England Merchants in the Seventeenth Century* (1955), ". . . characteristic of a whole class of Englishmen now beginning to arrive in the colonies. These men—customs functionaries, lesser bureaucrats, fortune hunters in official positions—found careers for themselves in the quickly expanding colonial administration."

Randolph's career in America was focused on the New England region, especially Massachusetts Bay. The status of that Puritan colony was threatened by the new imperialists, for upon the goal of bringing ordered relationships between the parent state and the Bay Province hinged much of the imperialists' hopes for the consolidation and unification of all the American colonies. This unique attention to Massachusetts was prompted partly by the fact that the Bay Colony, the hub of the northern possessions, determinedly maintained a posture of independence that mocked the new regulations and threatened failure for the imperialists.

In matters of commerce, the Massachusetts people had demonstrated an unwillingness to comply with Parliament's first attempts at trade regulation during Cromwell's years. And there was more to the Bay Province's attitude than merely the desire to continue profitable trading outside imperial regulations. The Bay people had questioned the authority of Parliament to legislate concerning their trade, and presumably any other matter, resting their interpretation of their constitutional guarantees on their 1629 charter from Charles I.

Thus, among his early actions, in 1664 Charles II had dispatched a commission to New England to receive the "surrender" to his authority of the people there. The terms requested were not particularly severe, but Massachusetts continued its defiant attitude—and no "surrender" was forthcoming. Neighboring Rhode Island and Connecticut, undoubtedly relieved to have settled their problems in the charters of the previous years, prudently complied with the commissioners' requests; Massachusetts moved not one inch. As a result, the reports from the commission were highly critical of the Bay Province, complaining of violations of the Acts of Trade, limited voting privileges to members of the Puritan congregations, and competitive economic activities that threatened harm to England's own economy. Ordered to send representatives to England to answer the commissioners' charges, the Massachusetts authorities delayed action and for a full decade (while London burned in the Great Fire, England suffered the ravages of the plague and fought a war with the Dutch) escaped further attention.

But then, after ten years, the "breathing spell" ran out, and by the mid-1670s the deferred issues again were raised. In this new act of the drama, Edward Randolph played an integral role, for he had secured from the newly created Lords of Trade a commission as agent for inspecting the Massachusetts province. His reports to the Trade Lords formed the basis for actions against the province. The debate that ensued consumed eight years—years full of continued agitation both from Randolph and his allies in America and from the new imperialists in England, looking toward a cancellation of the Massachusetts charter and a reconstruction of the colony, probably as a royal province. These were years full of spirited defense by the Massachusetts authorities as they attempted to counter the threats against them.

The battle, for Massachusetts, was a losing one; decision after decision went against her. The colony's claims to New Hampshire were denied, and by 1679 the establishment of a royal government there ended all hopes that it might be retained. Similarly, the Bay Colony's claims to Maine were ruled invalid and only by purchasing the rights awarded other claimants was it possible for Massachusetts to continue her control there. Finally the worst blow of all fell when the Lords of

Trade initiated legal action in the Court of Chancery in England against the Massachusetts charter. That court ruled, in 1684, that the patent was forfeit, and independent Massachusetts was now at the mercy of the Crown, with no chartered rights at all.

After the reduction of the charter, it might have been expected that Massachusetts would be restructured as a royal province, like Virginia, but the course of events in England altered that possibility. Charles II died in 1685 and was succeeded on the throne by his brother, James II. As proprietor of New York, James had gained some definite ideas about the proper reconstruction of the northern parts of his American empire. During the first year of his rule, imperial reorganization and the drive toward consolidation of the American empire reached its highest level of experimentation. Rather than merely bringing Massachusetts under direct royal control, there was now instituted a comprehensive revision of the entire governing structure for the northern colonies in the instrument termed the Dominion of New England.

The dominion was to include all of the New England colonies—New Hampshire, Massachusetts, Rhode Island, Plymouth, and Connecticut—as well as New York and New Jersey, with plans to include Pennsylvania eventually as well. Over this dominion was to be placed a royally appointed governor, who would be aided in his administration by a lieutenant governor and an appointed council. No provision was included for representative colonial assemblies. The elected legislative houses of the various colonies were abolished, with direct control from England to be instituted.

In terms of England's objectives, her theories of empire, and the desires of the imperialists dedicated to those theories and goals, the dominion made sense. But the plan ignored the historical and current realities of the American colonies, and to succeed would require both enlightened administration and time. Neither of these elements proved to be present. Sir Edmund Andros, the governor of the dominion, upon whom so much of its success or failure would depend, was lacking in the patience and tact necessary to forward intelligently the aims of the reorganization. And time, perhaps the most essential of ingredients, proved to be equally nonexistent. Within three years James would flee from England, allowing in the moment termed the Glorious Revolution the reestablishment of the monarchy in a new form, under the sovereigns, William III and his wife, Mary. Those events in England would see their counterparts in the New World as the Glorious Revolution helped spawn a series of smaller revolts in the American colonies, washing away the reorganized structure of imperial control as swiftly as the revolution in England had erased the Catholic rule of James II.

A REBELLION IN VIRGINIA

The last quarter of the seventeenth century was a time for testing the machinery of imperial control that had been fabricated since midcentury. It was also a time of continuous refinement and extension of those imperial policies, leading to the attempted consolidation in the Dominion of New England. Empire building had become a two-way street, with American reactions to English policies becoming an increasingly significant element in the workings of the imperial machinery. By the end of the century, it was obvious that the English empire not only would be shaped by policymakers in the homeland, but would also be modified in form and function by the realities of American colonial life. The results, in many instances, were compromises.

Clarence Ver Steeg, in *The Formative Years, 1607–1763* (1964), has suggested a fruitful way of looking at the colonists' reactions to imperial policies during this era. He sees the Americans entering a time of "social instability"; he views these as years when a colonist's place in his community and society was not clearly charted, and his actions reflected the uncertainty with which he confronted both present and future. It was a time of awkward adolescence. The Americans had succeeded in sustaining themselves during the difficult, hazardous years of colonizing; they had taken on the local economic and social characteristics. But the early founding generation was now gone. In its place were the sons and daughters of the founders (augmented, of course, by many newcomers) struggling to set patterns and control events in such a way that their particular objectives might be obtainable and that the promise of the "good life," freed from the restrictions of the Old World, might be brought to fruition in the New World. In the early years, it had been expected that life in America would be patterned on the English model, but by 1680 there were colonists who had never known England. This fact, along with the necessary adjustments caused by the American environment, had created a situation in which older social structures were withering away as new ones were in the process of creation.

This same freeing of men from previous concepts of well-ordered relationships, where "each man knew what was expected of him," has been described by Daniel Boorstin in *The Americans: The Colonial Experience* (1958) as a major promise of New World life, imparting an essential ingredient to the flavor of America. It was what most sharply distinguished colonial society from life in England. But the moments of recognition that the old was changing, the new arriving—exactly those last two decades of the seventeenth century when a generation of Americans searched for patterns not clearly discernible—are the years Ver Steeg describes as particularly characterized by social instability.

What happened in empire building during those years was conditioned by events in both England and America. For America it was a time of uncertainty and trouble. In the twenty years from 1675 to 1695, colonial life was beset by a variety of discordant episodes, including Indian wars, economic disloca- tions, the Salem witch hunt, and a series of rebellions—against a royal governor in Virginia, against proprietary rule in Maryland, against the newly instituted Dominion of New England in Massachusetts and New York. Historians studying the events of those years have become increasingly aware of the complexity of troublesome elements. In no one instance is it possible to relate a single-track story of English regulations opposed by militant American colonists who objected to those controls, revolted against them, and began, a century before its time, the prologue to the American Revolution. These were seventeenth-century crises, of a different sort from those that would come in the next century. But in the "unhinged" condition of American society, in the disorganized state of political groupings, in the disunified attitudes of colonists toward English policies are to be found some of the complex reasons for the local divisions that, when confronted with personalities and policies of imperial change, created the variety of American responses to the new empire.

In the events in Virginia of the years 1676–1677, the influence of the mother country's policies can be observed in two of the elements that led to Bacon's Rebellion. One of these was the constitutional fact that the appointed royal governor of the province, Sir William Berkeley, stood as the king's representative in Virginia, with his powers and authority derived from his royal commission and instructions. This, however, was not a determining factor among the forces shaping the rebellion, for it appears to have been Berkeley's use of his authority, his personal decisions within that large area allowed to him to form policies, rather than his constitutional powers, that some of the rebelling colonists objected to. The revolt may have been anti-Berkeley, but it does not appear to have been anti-English.

The second feature of the episode directly related to the empire was derived from the impact of the navigation laws on the economy of Virginia. Tobacco had been enumerated, and thus could be exported only to ports within the empire under the terms of the Navigation Act of 1660. Tobacco was also one of the American products most affected by the prohibition against colonial exportation in foreign vessels. The profitable trade the Virginians had enjoyed with Dutch carriers, especially during the years of the Interregnum, became illegal. The Virginia tobacco economy declined, although how much that decline resulted from shipping shortages occasioned by the prohibition on foreign vessels, or from enumeration, or from overproduction within Virginia, is debatable. At any rate, so far as economic depression was a cause of Bacon's Rebellion, and to the extent that Virginians believed the restrictions of the trade acts responsible for the falling price of tobacco (and this they seem to have done), the episode can be seen as an anti-imperial outbreak.

The causes of the uprising must be sought primarily within Virginia. The rebellion has been particularly studied by two historians who are far from agreement in their assessment of events. Their disagreement rests upon their judgments of the major protagonists in the troubles—the leader of the rebellion, Nathaniel Bacon, and the royal governor, Sir William Berkeley.

To Thomas Jefferson Wertenbaker, who presented his interpretation in a variety of publications, including a book entitled *Torchbearer of the Revolution* (1940), Bacon is the hero of the era, a true forerunner of the Patriots of 1776, who championed liberty endangered by English restrictions sponsored by tired, old, reactionary William Berkeley. In Wertenbaker's view, Bacon was a somewhat reluctant, but nonetheless true leader of the oppressed Virginia citizenry, a people downtrodden by a governor who ruled the province for fifteen years without elections, proved inept at Indian diplomacy, and was unable to defend the frontier settlements against raids by tribesmen; a royal governor who misused his powers to reward his friends and himself, caring little for the rest of the Virginia population.

Bacon, the young hero, led his citizen band against the arbitrary system Berkeley had fastened upon the Old Dominion, and finally died in the struggle. While nothing could save the leader from his untimely death, or those of his followers who were executed by Berkeley after he had regained power, vindication for the rebels came with the arrival of a royal commission to investigate the affair, the recalling of Berkeley to England, and, especially, the events of a century later when other Virginians—Washington, Jefferson, Henry, the Lees—joined their fellow colonists in America to wage another rebellion in the name of and for the cause of freedom. "Let us not forget," writes Wertenbaker, "that though the sun of American liberty sank blood red across the James as the old governor sent one patriot after another to the gallows, it was the same sun which rose a century later to shine down upon the triumph of the man we call the Father of His Country."

Against this version of the events in Virginia, 1676–1677, consider the findings of another scholar, Wilcomb E. Washburn, whose study *The Governor and the Rebel* (1957) presents the same episode in quite a different light. Washburn emphasizes the

Virginia frontiersman's aggressiveness in Indian policy, the role of a popular Governor Berkeley in attempts to limit the acquisitive drive for land and Indian spoliation, the shifting social, economic, and political status of large and ordinary planters, as well as economic depression and the personality conflicts coloring the Bacon-Berkeley relationships. But in all this, says Washburn, Bacon was no liberal leader of a leveling movement, Berkeley no tyrant exercising despotic powers over a half-enslaved people. And, for our purposes here, the revolt, in this view, was certainly not an anti-English uprising, not in origins and especially not in results.

Even so, one final note might be appended. Wesley Frank Craven, in *The Southern Colonies in the Seventeenth Century* (1949), has suggested that "by no means the least significant feature of Bacon's Rebellion" was the speed with which the English government reacted to the news from Virginia and the dispatching, along with a special commission of investigation, of an expedition of eleven vessels and more than 1,100 soldiers under the command of Berkeley's successor, Colonel Herbert Jeffreys. The arrival in Virginia of this force constituted an impressive symbol of the new imperial power, which must have been apparent to the colonists. Independence certainly was not an issue in Virginia at the time, yet the quickness of the royal response displays a sensitivity in imperial relationships indicative of the new empire. "Thoughtful men must have recognized that these soldiers represented a purpose destined to have enduring influence on the life of the colony."

OTHER REBELLIONS

About the time that Bacon's uprising in Virginia was challenging the authority of Governor Berkeley, the New England communities found themselves involved in the most serious Indian uprising in their history. King Philip's War taxed the financial and military resources of the New England colonies severely before the conflict had run its course. Yet, although distressingly disruptive, it was only one of several calamities visiting the northern colonies at the time. Hard on its heels came the depressing news of Massachusetts's loss of New Hampshire, the adverse decision regarding the Bay Colony's claims to Maine, the loss of the Massachusetts charter, and, finally, the institution of the Dominion of New England.

As Bacon's Rebellion in Virginia had demonstrated social instability in that province, so the arrival of the dominion governor, Sir Edmund Andros, and his imposition of the new order in Massachusetts Bay, exposed uncertainties and divisions within that colony. Bernard Bailyn, in his study of *The New England Merchants in the Seventeenth Century*, has shown that the events leading to the overthrow of Andros and his dominion were far from simple contests between liberty-loving Americans and a tyrannically arbitrary dominion governor. Bailyn has demonstrated the divisions within Massachusetts and the dichotomy between the older, inwardly oriented Puritan leadership, resisting change and determined to return as nearly as possible to the "Golden Age" of Massachusetts's independence (c. 1630–1660), on the one hand, and the interests and inclinations of newly rising men, many of them merchants, who could see the future welfare of the colony, and their own personal well-being, related to an extended role for Massachusetts within the framework of the English empire.

Massachusetts as a closed society, apart from the mainstream of the Western world, constantly purifying and building ever closer to God's Zion on earth, was not the sort of community to appear hospitable to a merchant group interested in widening its contacts and markets in the world at large. While profits and personal welfare, in theory, might be more easily attained in a nonregulated world, the realities of the emerging imperial structure led some merchants to believe it better to "do business" within the imperial limitations than obstinately attempt to rebuild the older version of the society.

Given such circumstances, Governor Andros could have solicited allies with whom to erect the Dominion of New England, but his lack of political sense, and the sudden toppling of his king in England, proved too much for him and his regime. Within the short time of his governorship, he had alienated some Bay dwellers by instituting Anglican church services, others by tightening the regulation of commerce, many by reexamining land titles. So the news of the Glorious Revolution at home was all the signal needed by the Bay people. They soon had Andros in prison, a manifesto justifying their "revolution" issued, and the colony, as an interim device, returned to its former political structure.

Similarly, in another part of the dominion, hostility to the new regime and local social circumstances produced rebellion. The Glorious Revolution in New York was more bloody than the events in Massachusetts. Yet Lawrence Leder, who analyzes the Leisler Revolt in New York, in *Robert Livingston and the Politics of Colonial New York, 1654–1728* (1961), is impressed by patterns similar to those found in Massachusetts. It was not, in his view, a class struggle of "haves" against "have nots" that brought Jacob Leisler to the leadership of New York affairs after the collapse of the dominion government. Nor was it that simple a division that accounts for the harshness of the reaction to Leisler's assumption of power (including the execution of Leisler and his lieutenant, Jacob Milborne) by the forces of a "restored" aristocracy. Rather than seeing Leisler as the leader of the downtrodden lower class, eagerly breaking the restraints around them, Leder's analysis emphasizes the basic collision as one between aristocrats and would-be aristocrats, between a relatively small group of men who wielded power and another relatively small group who wanted to assume that power.

But, again, the course of empire did not rest solely on internal, provincial factions or the results of their contests. Contributing to developments in New York, as in Massachusetts, was the reaction of Americans to the consolidating attempts of James II, and the fall of the dominion in New York, as in Massachusetts, disrupted the effort by England to order its northern colonies more completely and more rigidly into the orbit of empire.

The trio of uprisings in America that occurred at least partly because of radical events in England in 1688–1689 ended with an episode in the proprietary of Maryland. Here, as in neighboring Virginia's Bacon's Rebellion, it is more difficult to see the new imperial regulations as a major element in the origins of revolt. Rather, internal conditions within Maryland itself were the primary ingredients in the explosion—the long-standing antagonisms between Catholic and Protestant settlers, the seemingly unshakable policy of the proprietor of maintaining a Catholic governing group in office, the feudal-type landholding, and the inadequate Indian policies. The rebellion, when it came, fed on fears of an attempt by the deposed James II to establish a beachhead of Catholicism in Maryland. Together these elements led the Protestant Association, headed by John Coode, to crush the proprietary regime and create an interim structure to serve as Maryland's government until the new monarchs' will was known.

Thus, as of 1689–1690, the decades of imperial planning, the movement toward consolidation and regulation, had ended strangely. Virginia remained largely untouched by the Glorious Revolution, and uprisings that engulfed Carolina seem to have been relatively unrelated to events in England. But most of the mainland American provinces were in an awkward state. All of those former governments encompassed within the short-lived Dominion of New England, as well as the deposed proprietary of Maryland and its neighbor, Pennsylvania (for William Penn's relations with James II, along with other charges, were used by his enemies to shear him of his proprietary rights), remained in an unsettled condition, awaiting the decisions of the new monarchs about their overseas possessions. As David S. Love-joy, in *The Glorious Revolution in America* (1972), explains: "William and Mary were presented with a number of colonial governments in America they were unaware they had lost. England's revolution was imported by its colonists before some Englishmen had accepted it at home. Presumptuous Americans moved rapidly to satisfy provincial needs by exploiting a revolution which occurred at an opportune moment."

RESHAPING THE EMPIRE

Restructuring the empire was one of many problems facing the new Protestant monarch of England after the Glorious Revolution. Since William III had accepted the English throne partly because he planned to bring that kingdom to the aid of the League of Augsburg in its war against Louis XIV of France, the affairs of England now took on a military cast. Establishing himself in his new kingdom and preparing for war in Europe absorbed most of the new king's energies; colonial problems necessarily were considered only when domestic and European affairs allowed. But in time William and his advisers turned to the two major questions posed by the revolutionary events in the colonies. There was, first, the question of overall imperial structure—whether the basic aims of empire developed in the previous decades were to be altered, continued, expanded. And then, in a more specialized sense, it was necessary to consider the constitutional structure of each of those mainland colonies whose actions in the past months had ended the legitimately constituted government and which must be returned, in one fashion or another, to some stable arrangement.

The answer to the first of these questions demonstrated the deep-seated commitment of the English people to the basic tenets of mercantilistic thought which had brought the imperial structure to the time of the Glorious Revolution. As the Restoration in 1660 had not altered the basic structure begun during the Cromwellian years, so now the passage of the throne from James II to William III brought no alteration in the aims of the empire. In fact, given the sudden turn in foreign policy to direct contest with France, strategic benefits of the empire took on additional significance, extending the drive for imperial controls beyond the economic and social motivations of the past.

Two specific actions within the decade following the Glorious Revolution demonstrated these continued commitments to empire. William replaced the committee of the Privy Council responsible for supervision of colonial affairs, the Lords of Trade, with a new agency called the Board of Trade. Established as a combination of high-ranking noblemen and colonial experts, this fifteen-man board took over the functions of the older agency and became, at least in theory, the central agency for administering colonial affairs. At about the same time the structure of the empire was further defined by

Parliament in the comprehensive Navigation Act of 1696. This legislation continued the basic regulations of previous statutes and looked to more efficient enforcement of those laws with specific requirements for registration of commercial vessels, oaths from all colonial governors promising vigilant administration of the laws of trade, and the establishment of vice-admiralty courts within the colonies. These courts would provide opportunity for trials of accused violators outside the regular colonial courts, away from jury trials by neighbors reluctant to convict their fellow colonists for infringements of the imperial regulations.

On the other question—the reestablishment of legitimate governments within the individual colonies—William's decisions can be classed as rather middle-of-the-road settlements. The alternatives he might have considered ranged from, on the one hand, allowing the reestablishment of quasi-independent communities such as had existed before the Restoration in 1660 and, on the other, again attempting to institute consolidated government, perhaps another Dominion of New England. Instead, William moved in the direction of approximating relationships of the mid-1670s, thereby ensuring a perpetuation of the various structures that had characterized the American plantations. In fact, as Wesley Frank Craven explains, in *The Colonies in Transition, 1660–1713* (1968), "it is difficult to define any broad lines of policy [for reestablishment of colonial governments] that are not best stated in negative terms." While there would continue to be impulses toward uniformity, especially a determination to reduce all of the colonies to royal status, for the moment (and certainly partly as a result of the military necessities of that war period) the Crown was content to allow a basic reversion to older arrangements.

This meant that the reconstituted governments in each of the mainland American colonies would be formed on the basis of past history, in an individual way. New Hampshire would revert to its form when created in 1679, a province on the model of Virginia, with a royally appointed governor and council and an elected lower house of assembly. Rhode Island and Connecticut, emerging from the defunct dominion, contended that their post-Restoration charters were still valid. Successful in their claims, they were restored as corporate, chartered communities. Massachusetts also waged a vigorous defense of its rights to its old charter, but without success. Imperial considerations, and past history, necessitated some alterations and the result was a new charter, issued in 1691.

Massachusetts, under its new patent, would have a royally appointed governor and a council composed in a unique fashion, with the members nominated by the elected house of assembly, subject to confirmation by the governor. The franchise in the province now was to rest on property, rather than religious qualifications. Legislation of the Massachusetts General Court was subject to review and possible disallowance by the Crown. The arrangements were something of a compromise, midway between the desires of the Massachusetts colonials to return to their 1629 charter and the suggestions of those in England who argued for a total reduction of the province to royal status.

New York, set free from proprietary and dominion control, was made a royal province on the Virginia model, with appointed governor and council and, after long years without the privilege, an elected lower house of assembly. The other part of the former Dutch conquest, now severed from the original proprietors and in the hands of capitalist landlords, would become the royal province of New Jersey shortly after the turn of the century.

The drive to reduce the Penn and Calvert proprietaries met a similar end. William Penn was deprived of his governing rights in Pennsylvania for two years (1692–1694), but he regained his chartered powers and he and his heirs would retain those rights until the time of the American Revolution. As for Maryland, the Crown assumed political authority but allowed the economic benefits of the proprietary to remain in Calvert control. This arrangement lasted until 1715 when the political rights were restored to the proprietor.

Virginia's structure had not been upset by the events of the time, and the Old Dominion needed no specific reorganization. The Carolina proprietors retained their charter and moved to reassert their control. Later, in the coming century, the rights of seven of the eight grantees were purchased by the Crown (the eighth received a special grant of lands in North Carolina), and Carolina, by then divided permanently into its northern and southern parts, became royal provinces. As for the borderlands south of Carolina, it was not until the 1730s that the effort to erect the outpost called Georgia got under way.

By the end of the seventeenth century, then, the empire had been put back together after its Humpty-Dumpty-like fall. In the first six decades of the century ahead, the English would pursue their national goals, building internal strength, waging expensive but ultimately victorious war with France and other enemies, and directing affairs of empire in such a way that the goals of domestic well-being, security, and prestige all progressed. And in America, during those same six decades, the colonists would experience economic, population, social, and cultural growth, emerging at the end of the era as something unique in world experience—a new people, operating within a novel framework of social organization. But at no time during those first six decades of the eighteenth century did England ever systematically attempt to reshape the empire to conform with the consolidated, uniform system that remained the theoretical empire ·in the minds of some Englishmen. Rather, an ever-widening division grew between the theories of empire as they had been defined in the seventeenth century and the actual working realities between parent state and colonies as they developed in the century that followed.

TWO

The Economic Empire

Of all aspects of the first British Empire, no other has so concerned American historians as the economic regulations of the old imperial system, codified in the laws known as the Acts of Trade and Navigation. A description of those laws has satisfied some historians as a description of the imperial connection between colonies and mother country. For other students of America's early years, an evaluation of the effect of those laws upon colonial development has been sufficient to characterize the general effects of imperial ties with Great

Britain. The one central question that has long engaged the historians' curiosity and talents concerning the origins of the United States has been: How did the British imperial system affect the American colonies? Other questions follow in close order: Were the economic regulations an obvious example of British "tyranny" over freedom-seeking Americans, as George Bancroft asserted in the nineteenth century? Or was the first British Empire a well-balanced, reciprocal arrangement economically, in which the colonies as well as the mother country prospered, as George L. Beer, Charles M. Andrews, and other "imperialist" historians writing in the late nineteenth and early twentieth centuries stated? Are such "imperialists" wrong in their pleasant pictures of mutual benefits, as Louis Hacker and other historians of the 1930s and 1940s asserted, emphasizing instead the competitive nature of the British mercantile capitalists and their counterparts within the colonies? Or are the evaluations of Oliver M. Dickerson and Lawrence H. Gipson—who viewed the Americans as peculiarly blessed by the economic and other advantages derived from the imperial connection—closer to historical truth? Is Dickerson correct in his assumption that Americans voiced little objection to the navigation system because it was benign, or is Thomas Barrow's assertion that objections were limited because the restraints were so laxly enforced a more credible suggestion?

Before turning to the specific question of the impact of the empire upon colonial life, certain general facets of the imperial relationship warrant description, so that a proper perspective may be maintained when considering specifics. Otherwise, some of the more significant aspects of the economic empire will be forgotten or misleadingly reduced in importance.

First, it should be noted that, in addition to imperial regulation, many other elements shaped the colonial economy, including such variables as the availability of investment capital, the supply and cost of labor, the constantly shifting economic climate produced by wartime or peacetime needs, the expanding population, and the changing endeavors to utilize profitably the natural resources of the colonies. Unless these and at times other variables are included in an evaluation, historically misleading conclusions may result from any attempt to interpret the significance of imperial regulation.

Second, imperial regulation most obviously and directly affected mercantile and industrial pursuits, yet the colonial economies were based, in very large measure, not upon commerce or industry, but rather upon agriculture. The overwhelming majority of Americans, perhaps some 90 percent of the total working population, earned its daily sustenance directly from agricultural endeavors. In the pattern of economic life of each productive colonist, mercantile activities (as well as the few nascent industries and such extractive enterprises as fur gathering, lumbering, and fishing) were less directly related to the daily struggle for survival than the production of agricultural goods. Thus it is of some significance that, although indirectly the imperial economic system and agriculture were intertwined, the impact of the trade laws could be experienced directly by only a limited fraction of the total colonial population.

Given the overriding significance of agriculture in the colonial economies, the process for securing and holding real estate becomes central to any analysis of economic development. While exceptions to the rule may be cited here and there, for the most part land acquisition was not an imperially regulated enterprise in the eighteenth century. There were sectional and regional differences in the way private individuals gained and held agricultural land, but generally the entire procedure was locally (that is, provincially) controlled. In the seventeenth century, while vast proprietary grants were being patented and provincial governments structured, imperial decisions often directly affected landholding. But in the eighteenth century, as governments stabilized and, except for Georgia, the major severances of the Crown's domains were completed, there was less and less opportunity for any imperial process for land acquisition to be imposed.

The provincial governments, whether chartered, proprietary, or royal, devised their own operations for land granting, and the ease or difficulty of obtaining land titles depended primarily upon the dominant political group's intentions and objectives. While it is true that in the plantation colonies of the South, particularly in South Carolina and Virginia, and in the former Dutch province of New York, large estates worked against the characteristics, the basic pattern of landholding in British North America was one of small holdings, individually cultivated, upon relatively free tenure. It was this fact that made life in the British colonies the dream of so many immigrants of the eighteenth century. In contrast to the world they knew in Britain, in Ireland, or on the continent of Europe, America was a limitless expanse of productive agricultural land, where the self-sufficient individual might attain goals of personal welfare forever closed to him in the land-poor Old World.

This promise, actually obtainable in the colonies, was in only minor ways directly interfered with by official British actions. During the years before 1763, in fact, if there was an official British policy concerning land acquisition, it was often directed toward a continuation and advancement of small landholding. The imposition of quit rents (annual fees levied without regard to improvements upon land held of the king or proprietor) was encouraged by Britain. In addition to their obvious advantage as revenue producers, they tended to discourage acquisition of or speculation in large, unimproved tracts of land. Working in counterdirection, it is true, the grants, late in the era, of trans-Appalachian lands to syndicates or land companies tended to further the opposite trend. But, in balance, British imperial regulations or, in most instances, the lack of them, allowed the widespread holding of real property in the colonies and the shaping of a society characterized by "middle-class" agriculturalists.

Curtis P. Nettels (*The Roots of American Civilization*, 2d ed., 1963) has pointed out that, insofar as such a policy existed, the concept of small landholdings did complement the basic tenets of mercantilism, for the production of goods from small holdings would increase commerce and thus work to advance the trade of the empire. Land in small lots, diligently cultivated, prospered commerce, while land in large, unsettled tracts, held speculatively until social needs pushed values upward, contributed little or nothing to trade. The British policy of encouraging the peopling of the colonies—first from Britain and later from the continent of Europe—worked toward the same ends, for large populations in the dominions would increase the trade of the empire and further develop national strength. Until about the 1680s English mercantilists viewed emigration from the homeland to the colonies as a blessing, for it siphoned excess labor from England. But later, analysis of the home economy brought a change. Fearing too much weakening of the home labor force from such emigration, imperialists now stressed the advantages of immigration to America from continental Europe and from the more mature American colonies into the newer settlements. In both instances, however, the goal was the same, and the spectacular increases in colonial population during the eighteenth century attested to the success of the policy of encouragement—a policy indicated by various decisions and instructions from the Board of Trade and Parliamentary legislation which stipulated relatively easy naturalization of alien immigrants.

Imperial planners also attempted to fashion colonial economic ventures into a complementary rather than competitive place in the empire. In an entirely natural way, British imperial theorists saw benefits from colonies producing goods unavailable in the homeland, thus reducing dependence upon other nations for needed or desired goods. The list of such products ranged from sugar and cotton to tobacco, rice, and indigo, to naval stores and ship timbers, wine, and silk. The records of imperial planning contain widely differing results. In some instances, notably indigo and naval stores, the policies were quite successful, as will be noted in greater detail later. Other experiments, especially the efforts to stimulate wine and silk culture, ended as discouraging failures. No amount of imperial prodding, it seems, could overcome more powerful determinants, such as the scarcity of laborers skilled in those enterprises and, perhaps even more significant, the fact that greater, quicker, and more certain returns could be realized from other agricultural endeavors.

It made little difference whether or not the originators of a colony intended for agriculture to be dominant; the events of the early years in most of the mainland plantations demonstrated that permanence and stability could be assured only by a colony's ability to sustain itself through local food production. Dependence upon a home base in England for supplies proved much too hazardous. Thus agricultural production, in its earliest form, was directed to crops needed to sustain the newly planted outpost. Only after the colony's immediate needs were satisfied was time and energy available to develop exportable surpluses.

But, having satisfied those initial needs, the American colonies could, and did, move into the more advanced state of production, harvesting surpluses which, in turn, required transportation to increasingly widespread markets. Thus agriculture, in its secondary stage in the colonies, generated the commercial sector of the economy. Commerce, it is true, had been evolving through impetus from fur trading and from fishing and, to a lesser extent, lumbering, for all of these extractive enterprises had produced cargoes for extracolonial markets. It was, however, the success of the Americans in expanding their farms and plantations that formed the basic foundations for the general expansion of the colonial economy during the eighteenth century, coupled as it was with the Americans' ability to seek out and develop markets in which to dispose profitably of those agricultural products. And it is at this point, when agricultural goods entered into commerce outside the colony of production, that the colonists were brought most directly into contact with the commercial regulations of the empire, more specifically the Acts of Trade and Navigation.

SHIPPING AND STAPLES

As stated at the beginning of this chapter, the question of the impact of the navigation acts upon the American colonial economy has been a favorite topic for analysis, discussion, and argument among historians for many years. There are several reasons why this has been so. For one thing, the topic is central in attempting to assess motivations for the American Revolution, and the efforts to measure the effects of regulation after 1763 has drawn historians into the colonial era, seeking antecedents of the policies of the mother country, and American reactions to those policies, of the Revolutionary years. Another reason is that, throughout the years since the Americans left the British Empire, debate over specific commercial policies and general national economic regulations has flourished. Those debates ranged from the nineteenth-century discussions about free trade to American contests over tariff policies; from Panama Canal regulations to the European Common Market. In all of these debates, "history" has been sought as a weapon to prove virtues or defects of regulated commercial systems.

It is probably also true that a study of imperial trade regulations is in some ways easier to engage in, less abstract in definition and involving data seemingly more manageable, than some other aspects of the first British Empire. The trade laws, in basic form, were statutes of Parliament, words capable of scholarly analysis. Revenue receipts were recorded; port entrances and clearances, as well as merchants' papers, survive to be studied. Compared with concepts which are more difficult to define, such as (to cite only a single example) the psychology of a colonial population, the economic empire may be examined with more ordinary tools of scholarship. Yet it is interesting that Lawrence A. Harper ("The Effect of the Navigation Acts on the Thirteen Colonies" in *The Era of the American Revolution*, Richard B. Morris, ed. [1939]), after concluding that the colonists paid a heavy price under the system for the benefits they received from Britain (a conclusion emphatically rejected by other scholars), cautioned against assuming this automatically implied that the trade laws were a major determinant in the American decision to revolt against British rule. As Harper warned, any simple "cost accounting, balance sheet" (the words are mine, not his) approach to the question may be historically misleading, for regardless of what modern computers may tell us about the cost of imperial connection, the colonists acted from their own interpretations of what they themselves believed and experienced. The empire existed for more than three generations before American resistance created the crisis of revolution. Harper reminds us that human beings learn, over a period of time, to live under undesirable or unprofitable restraints.

Statistical, customs-house history alone can never tell us with precision the actual impact of imperial membership. Most students of the American colonies and the British Empire have been aware of the limitations Harper warns against, and have cast their historical nets widely. Yet some studies of the question have been, and probably always will be, predicated on the primacy of statistical analysis, emphasizing the "costs" and "dividends" of the imperial connection.

One such attempt is Robert Paul Thomas, "A Quantitative Approach to the Study of the Effects of British Imperial Policy upon Colonial Welfare: Some Preliminary Findings," *The Journal of Economic History* 25 (December 1965). The models Thomas uses are the estimated annual averages for the period 1763–1772 and for the single year 1770; he ventures the hypothesis that "membership in the British Empire, after 1763, did not impose a significant hardship upon the American colonies." Although this relates to years beyond the limits of this book, comparable studies might yield similar findings for earlier decades. And such studies promise to become increasingly sophisticated. The work of James F. Shepherd and Gary M. Walton in *Shipping, Maritime Trade, and the Economic Development of Colonial North America* (Cambridge, England, 1972) provides analysis and supporting statistical evidence upon which studies of the effects of trade policies and other economic determinants may be based.

In turning to an actual examination of what historians have concluded from their investigations of the nature of the economic empire, it is necessary to caution against an either-or, blanket-type description. Most modern scholars concede that the imperial regulations Britain instituted were neither totally harmful nor totally beneficial to America, the proper assessment lying somewhere in between. Of course, in attempting to locate the precise point within that "middle ground," there is room for historians to disagree.

The departure point for a general examination of the problem might well be the findings of Oliver M. Dickerson, who, in 1951, reported the conclusions of a detailed investigation of the colonial system in a book entitled *The Navigation Acts and the American Revolution.* Building on, but revising and modifying, previous findings, particularly those of George L. Beer and Lawrence A. Harper, Dickerson addressed himself to the central question: How oppressive were the navigation acts? The answers he found form the first half of his book. His conclusions are buttressed both by detailed analyses of the trade laws in operation and by his study of the attitudes of American colonists toward those laws. In general, he finds little in the system to condemn. He sees the American colonies prospering under the aegis of the British Empire; he views the imperial regulations as reciprocally beneficial to mother country and colonies; he reports negatively on his search for significant displays of American hostility to the imperial system; and he concludes that, until 1763, the colonists lived in, if not the best of all economic worlds, at least a very good one, in which both they and their parent state developed increasing prosperity, all a result of the economic regulations. "For one hundred years," Dickerson asserts, "the trade and navigation system had provided the most important cement of empire."

Dickerson's method of analysis is to examine the effects of each of the navigation acts on the colonies, arriving in the end at the conclusions summarized in the preceding paragraph. He begins with the Navigation Act of 1660, and finds that whatever adverse effects that legislation had generated during its first four decades was no longer a serious concern after 1700. This was the Parliamentary act that restricted the carrying trade of the empire to English and English-colonial vessels. Initially, at least, it had created a shortage of ships to handle American goods; foreign competitors, especially the Dutch, had been driven from the commerce and there were not enough English vessels to fill the vacuum created. In the past, scholars have charged that this freight shortage both increased freight rates and hampered the natural expansion of the American economy throughout most, if not all, of the colonial era. This condition, if it existed, would have constituted a significantly oppressive feature of regulation. But Dickerson answers that any such shortage of freight capacity was corrected by the beginnings of the eighteenth century; thus that part of the 1660 act did not affect freight rates after 1700.

Instead of viewing the 1660 act as harmful or oppressive to the colonists, Dickerson concludes that it actually helped the growth of the American economy in two distinct ways. First, it enhanced shipbuilding in the New World, for vessels built in the colonies (or owned and operated there) were classified as English ships within the definitions of the statute. In fact, Dickerson believes that this was directly responsible for the rising colonial shipbuilding industry, an industry which produced, by the time of the American Revolution, one-third the tonnage of ships registered under the British flag. Dickerson's enthusiasm is somewhat tempered by other historians who have pointed out that most of the American vessels were small sloops and schooners, used in coastal and West Indian commerce, while the bulk of the trans-Atlantic trade continued to be carried in the larger vessels built in Britain. This specialization in ship construction somewhat reduces the beneficial aspects of the Act of 1660 as Dickerson describes it. He asserts that the only colonial regions which could "theoretically" have found the limitation of the carrying trade to British vessels "even an imaginary grievance" were the plantation areas because after 1700, English, and particularly New England, shipping expanded so that there was ample capacity and competition for cargoes. But if the colonial-built shipping did not carry a large part of the trans-Atlantic trade, then the expansion of ship construction that answered the freight requirements of the southern provinces was British, not American. Even so, the development of the shipbuilding industry in the colonies was impressive, and the Act of 1660 helped to make it so.

Dickerson sees a second positive benefit from the legislation in its elimination of the hazards and uncertainties that foreign shipping would have created in the colonial economy, especially because of the many years of international warfare during the eighteenth century. Since the colonists were dependent upon overseas markets for their prosperity, chaos that might have resulted from dependence on foreign shippers was eliminated.

Stability, a requisite for economic development, was attained. War disrupted colonial commercial and, indirectly, agricultural and industrial life much less than it would have if "alien" carriage in peacetime had been allowed. As it was, British and colonial ships could continue their freight hauling, usually along trade lanes protected by the British navy. Thus Dickerson denies any burdensome result from the carrying clauses of the Act of 1660, arguing instead that colonial shipbuilding prospered and American commerce was stabilized as a result of the beneficial policy.

A second feature of the Navigation Act of 1660 (and later additions to that legislation) that Dickerson investigates is the policy of enumeration—that is, the designation of certain staple colonial products for shipment only to markets within the British Empire. If enumerated, the product had to be traded from its colony of origin to imperial ports, even though, in some cases, most of the goods eventually were reshipped to foreign consumer markets. There were three major mainland products that were enumerated: tobacco, rice, and indigo. These products, Dickerson states, did not have to be grown anywhere, yet the fact that they formed the economic base of the colonial South indicates that, even though enumerated, they were profitable—more profitable, probably, than alternative, unenumerated goods that the colonists might have produced. The choice, he explains, was the Americans'. Their continued concentration on enumerated products suggests that the market restrictions on them could not have been a controlling factor, oppressive to the colonists.

Considering each product individually, Dickerson first examines the tobacco industry. He reports that the production of tobacco in the Chesapeake region was full of risks and difficulties, but rather than linking these hazards with enumeration, Dickerson asserts that the basic problem was one that "commercial farmers" always face—the chronic condition of being in debt. Despite this, he views the tobacco industry as basically prosperous until the American Revolution. This, he says, was true not just of the tobacco planters, but of the entire economic structure dependent on the product—the shippers, the merchants, the financiers. In fact, he says, the proof of the benefits the structure dispensed can be seen in what happened to the industry after the Revolution, when for three-quarters of a century the American tobacco industry struggled to regain the stability and prosperity it had known as part of the British Empire. The heart of this system was the central British market, providing a focal point for the entire industry, bringing a needed, responsible measure of order to the American (production) side, the British (transportation, distribution, and financial) side and, for that large part of the product reshipped from Britain, to the European (consumer) side of the enterprise.

Not all historians would agree with this singularly pleasant picture of the colonial tobacco economy. Some scholars suggest that the American side of the industry declined in vigor during the closing years of the colonial era; that the tobacco region's vitality had weakened, despite the gloss of luxurious, credit-based living. They point to the increased tempo of agricultural diversification in both Virginia and Maryland as indicators of the tobacco planters' need to find stability in a more varied economic foundation, turning to wheat, hemp, and other crops to supplement their tobacco earnings. But diversification attempts were not limited to the last years of the old empire; resistance to and unhappiness with the concentration on tobacco are longstanding elements in the Chesapeake history. And the impetus for diversification often came from Britain, not the colonies. Despite this, tobacco remained "king," and with it British merchants flourished, Crown revenues increased, and American planters made money.

Some critics might say: Even if all this were true, wouldn't the Americans have made *more* money had they been free to trade their tobacco outside the empire—if tobacco, unregulated, had been freed from enumeration and the crushing burdens of imperial duties, merchants' warehousing charges and commissions for handling, especially since a large part of the crop was ultimately peddled in non-British markets? Not true, says Dickerson. The Americans could not have created a central market to replace that which existed in the British Isles. From this market came the benefits of capital financing and credit arrangements, experienced wholesaling, the general "know-how" essential to the entire industry. The proof, again, is apparent in the disorganized condition of the American tobacco industry after the Revolution. As far as tobacco is concerned (and it was by far the single most significant economic enterprise in the mainland colonies), Dickerson is certain that membership in the empire brought benefits far outweighing the burdens imposed by regulation.

Much the same patterns are visible in the rice industry, where again the world market (at least the *Western* world market) was located in Great Britain, to which the enumerated rice from America was sent. In this case, however, the colonists had been allowed a dispensation; the rice of Carolina and Georgia could be shipped directly to Mediterranean ports south of Cape Finisterre. Even so, according to Dickerson, more than half as much American rice was imported into southern Europe through the English market as was brought directly from America, demonstrating the value of that central market. When the Revolution eliminated the market in Britain and with it the financial benefits available to American planters, the rice industry of the United States rapidly declined.

The third enumerated staple crop from the mainland colonies was indigo. It was not only enumerated, but was also officially encouraged by the payment of a bounty on its export from the colonies to Britain. This vegetable derivative, so useful as a dye in the textile industry, had been developed in South Carolina during the eighteenth century and prospered there until the American Revolution. Then, as in the case of rice and tobacco, separation from the empire ended the profitability of indigo because, Dickerson explains, the imperial bounty was used to encourage the product in other parts of the empire, creating competition against which the American industry could not survive. Thus Dickerson sees this third major staple enterprise dependent upon its imperial encouragement, and while the advantages Britain gained from her policies are not denied, the story of colonial indigo amply demonstrates the benefits of the empire to the colonists.

THE NORTHERN COMMERCE

The enumerated products of major importance to the mainland colonies were all southern in origin. Because they formed the bulk of raw exports desired by the mother country, these products placed the plantation provinces in what imperial planners considered an ideal situation. Not only did they directly answer the needs of the nation, but their annual shipments of goods to Britain also provided the means whereby the southern colonists could purchase the fabricated goods brought back across the Atlantic each year. This trade was also regulated. The Staple Act of 1663 provided that goods imported into the colonies, either of English or northern European origin, must be cleared through a British port. While the charges for handling these shipments in Britain increased the price to consumers in the colonies, the southern provinces, with their yearly credits for their staple crops sent to Britain, could live and evidently prosper within the regulations. But the northern colonists, lacking exportable products needed in the homeland, faced a different situation.

The middle colonies, with their diversified agricultural surpluses, including increasing quantities of grain products, and the New England colonies both produced competitive, not complementary, exports for which there was no regular market at home. In order to develop their internal economies and to meet the necessary payments for fabricated goods imported from Britain (as the law required), markets in other parts of the world had to be developed. That the northern colonists were able to find such markets, and further their prosperity within the framework of imperial regulation, indicates something of the imaginative talents of the northern merchants. The need led to the development of intercolonial trading, to the opening and expanding of markets in southern Europe, and, above all, to the increasingly significant traffic between the northern mainland ports and the West Indian islands. Only by developing these markets were the northern merchants able to accumulate sufficient profits to continue to import desired goods from Britain.

In his study of the navigation acts, Dickerson acknowledges the significance of this trade, but he cautions about treating the separate areas of commerce as compartmentalized units, worrying about balances within each bilateral set of exchanges. Rather, he presents the alternative of viewing the total imperial trade as a single unit and asserts that, within this frame, both the mother country and the colonists prospered during the era.

While there is much to be said for this way of viewing the effects of regulation, there are some unanswered questions too. If the restrictions on importation of goods directly from England had not been imposed, might not the northern colonies have found satisfactory markets in a less hazardous way? Might not those markets have allowed their own agriculture and industry to develop more quickly and more fully? Certainly central to the forces shaping the patterns of northern colonial commerce was the need to garner the credits to pay for goods imported from Britain. And, although the northern merchants managed, through ingenuity and hard work, to profit from commerce within the regulations, perhaps they might have advanced more fully if such roundabout commercial patterns had not been required.

Then, too, while it may satisfy twentieth-century historians to view the imperial trade in its totality, it is quite obvious that some contemporary merchants and policymakers lacked that perspective in their own time. No matter how clearly today's scholar can see the interrelationships between the various segments of imperial commerce, to merchants and politicians then such connections were often obscured. A good example is the official attitude of Britain toward the increasing commerce between the northern colonies and the foreign West Indies.

The elements of this trade, in their simplest form, were: The Caribbean islands that produced sugar and its by-products were claimed by various European powers; some were English, some were French, some Dutch, some Spanish. In their search for markets, northern mainland merchants had found these islands places of profit. Single-crop areas, the islands particularly needed foodstuffs to feed their laboring force and timber products (barrels and casks) to package their export sugar products. Fish, beef and pork, staves, hoops and barrel heads were taken from the northern mainland ports to the islands and exchanged for sugar, molasses, and specie. The last two were the most important. The molasses was returned to the rum distilleries in the colonies; the specie provided the means of paying for goods imported from Britain.

Much of the prosperity of the northern mainland colonies depended upon this trade with the West Indies. It was obvious to many northern merchants, as it is to historians today, that any diminution of this trade would imperil the continued volume of imports from the mother country. Yet on occasion British imperial policy seemed to evince no genuine appreciation of this fact. When war erupted among European powers, British officials insisted that trade between the mainland colonies and the foreign enemy islands be halted. There might have been no problem had the British islands been able to absorb the mainland cargoes and satisfy the demand of the northern merchants for sugar products. But they could not, and thus the trade encompassed the French and other foreign islands. Trading with the enemy was looked upon in Britain in its narrowest sense as an act of disloyalty, without (Americans claimed) full appreciation of the hazards to the imperial economy that a disruption of such trading would entail.

Even more obvious, in Americans' eyes, as an indicator of the lack of comprehension of the ways imperial trade actually flowed was the Parliamentary enactment in 1733 of the legislation known as the Molasses Act. This was a peacetime measure, legislated in response to demands from the British West Indian sugar interests for protection against the competition they faced from the foreign islands. It imposed unreasonably heavy duties on foreign sugar products imported into the mainland colonies. To American mainlanders, it signified a sacrifice of their economic well-being for the economic security of the British islands.

Some historians, including Lawrence H. Gipson in *The British Empire before the American Revolution* (1936–1970), defend British action here by stressing the relative importance of the West Indies to Britain, compared with the lesser significance of the mainland colonies. It is also true that, in practice, the act was never enforced. Commerce in sugar products between foreign islands and the northern ports continued. In fact, Dickerson claims that even the British sugar interests in the West Indies did not desire enforcement of the act. But Gilman Ostrander ("The Colonial Molasses Trade," *Agricultural History* 30 [April 1956]) believes the effects of the legislation were harmful to the colonies on the mainland, for the act limited their search for trade and markets, arbitrarily attempting to sacrifice the profits of one part of the empire for the benefit of another.

Certainly the fact that the legislation was enacted should not be ignored in any general review of British imperial legislation, no matter how minimal its effect in shaping colonial commerce. For the very enactment indicates that, at best, the total pattern of imperial trade was not completely clear to British policymakers or, and in some ways even more revealing in the light of the colonists' charges, the welfare of one part of the empire might indeed be reduced in order to protect the interests of another part.

The generally accepted conclusion that the Molasses Act of 1733 never was effectively enforced leads directly to the larger question: How rigidly were all of the navigation acts administered? Evidence gathered, and interpretation drawn from the evidence, again seem to differ. One group of historians is convinced that evasion of the trade laws was an almost full-time occupation of the American colonists. They describe the trade laws as almost entirely lacking in real significance. In this view, the Americans continued to conduct commerce as they wished, without let or hindrance. In fact, scholars such as George L. Beer, who probably would have agreed with the more recent evaluations of Dickerson that the colonies flourished within the imperial structure, partly explained their opinions on the basis of the ineffectiveness of the laws in actual operation. A second view, shared by Dickerson and, earlier, Lawrence A. Harper (who believed that for this reason the laws might have been burdensome to the colonists), suggests the opposite, asserting that the great majority of American colonial trade was conducted within the channels set down by the trade laws, with only a few extralegal excursions, such as the practical nullification of the Molasses Act, occurring when compliance might have completely wrecked a segment of the colonial economy. Esmond Wright in *Fabric of Freedom: 1763–1800* (1961) sums up this viewpoint, stating that tea and molasses were the only commodities systematically smuggled into mainland ports.

Thomas Barrow (*Trade and Empire: The British Customs Service in Colonial America* [1967]) is not so certain the matter can be dismissed that easily. His listing of smuggled items is more extensive and includes gunpowder, paper, and luxury items. He admits that illicit trade ". . . was in the nature of a supplement to regular trade, the merchants adjusting their activities to the needs and the profits of the moment. At no point, except possibly in the frantic moments preceding the outbreak of the Revolution, did illicit trade even approach the legitimate English trade in volume or value." But, writes Barrow, "the major importance of illicit trade lay not in its volume but in its effect. The evidence suggests that the colonial merchants were restrained from such activities by the economic advantages of trade with England rather than by enforcement of the laws. When evasion was profitable, it was usually possible; the colonists could indulge in it with relative freedom. The consequences were serious, since a general disrespect for law was a logical result."

Then, too, perhaps what people thought was occurring was more important than what was actually happening. It seems that, at least on occasion, some of those in Britain responsible for planning and executing colonial policies assumed that Americans generally, and New Englanders in particular, operated outside the law on every possible occasion; that smuggling had become a distinctive American trait; and that this "fact" needed to be considered in all planning concerning the regulation of imperial trade.

INDUSTRIAL REGULATIONS

Besides the regulation of commerce within the empire, to ensure that strategic materials were not lost to foreign states and that the flow of goods within the empire protected the national interests, Britain also laid down regulations concerning industrial development within the American provinces. Some of these measures were intended to discourage the colonists from entering sectors of the economy where they would provide unwanted competition to home industries. Others were designed to encourage particular activities which would enhance the national interests by reducing Britain's dependence upon other parts of the world for desired or necessary commodities.

Those imperial regulations dealing with the indigo industry have been described above. Some historians believe that the industry's prosperity rested on the bounties paid by Britain. Encouragement was also given to those items directly used by the merchants in their sailing vessels and by the royal naval fleet: ship timbers, masts, naval stores, and hemp. The timber available in Britain for shipbuilding, especially the tall, broad trees needed for masts, was rapidly being depleted, and a new source was required. Naval stores—that is, pitch, tar, turpentine, and resin—all products of pitch pine forests, were ordinarily secured from the Baltic area, but reliance on this foreign source for strategic materials created hazards, especially in wartime. American sources for naval materials not only would keep the trade within the empire and further the goal of imperial self-sufficiency; it would also eliminate a dangerous dependence on foreign sources for vital materials.

The methods used to further this policy differed from product to product. In the case of masts and ship timbers, a rudimentary conservation policy was established by which tracts of standing timber, particularly in New England's extensive white pine forests, were set aside. These "King's Woods" became forest reserves, from which, under contract, sanctioned cuttings could take place. Naval stores, on the other hand, were treated in a method similar to indigo, with bounties paid on the export of American products to the homeland. The primary source of naval stores was developed in North Carolina.

In addition to encouraging products like indigo and naval stores with direct bounties, the shape of the economic empire was manipulated by restrictive legislation enacted in response to demands by British interest groups who felt threatened by competition, actual or potential, from the colonies. This type of regulation was specifically directed against three types of industrial products: woolen textiles, hats, and iron.

The earliest enactment was a law regulating woolens. Parliament, in 1699, attempted to reduce or eliminate competition to British woolen interests from both Irish and American producers. The law's impact was probably much greater in Ireland than in America, for a developing Irish textile industry posed an immediate threat to the English. It might, incidentally, be pointed out that there was a secondary effect of the law in Ireland. The depression of the industry there, following the imposition of the restrictions, was partly responsible for the immense emigration from northern Ireland to the American colonies in the eighteenth century.

In America, the effects of the legislation were less dramatic and probably less significant. The Woolens Act prohibited only the exportation of woolens by water from the place of production, so domestic commerce in locally made cloth was still permissible. But since, at the time of enactment, the colonial textile industry was still very much in its infancy and largely a domestic enterprise, at most the regulation could only keep a potential industry from developing. Whether, without the restrictions, a sizable colonial woolen industry ever would have developed is uncertain. Victor S. Clark, in *The History of Manufacturers in the United States* (1929), concluded there was little possibility of such development. Two basic elements seemed to work against it. Colonial labor was always a high-priced commodity, and it is doubtful if a textile industry could have attracted sufficient numbers of skilled workers. Also, as long as British woolens, which were superior products, could be obtained for lower prices than domestically made cloth, there was little reason to devote energy or capital to the colonial cloth industry. Thus, it is reasoned, the Woolens Act of 1699 had little actual effect on the development of the colonial economy.

The second industry to be regulated was hat manufacture. Again, the legislation (in 1732) was instigated by English manufacturers who feared the competition of American producers. In this case, the proscriptive legislation not only forbade the exportation of manufactured hats from the colony of origin by water; it also laid down rules restricting the number of apprentices in a hatmaking shop to no more than two and forbade contracting of Negro apprentices. Unlike the Woolens Act, these restrictions on hatmaking involved an industry that consumed raw materials (North American furs) from sources closer to colonial producers than to their English competitors.

Historians debate the effects of the legislation. Dickerson, for example, believes that, although there might have been a "temporary effect" on the development of an export trade in hats from New England, the overall effect was not serious, for it was "more advantageous" for hatmakers to move around the colonies, plying their trade from place to place, than it would have been for them to establish permanent shops. On the other hand, Lawrence A. Harper has calculated that, among all the industrial regulations, the Hat Act probably came closest to ruining a young American industry that was reasonably well developed in the northern colonies. Before the enactment, New York and New England hatters were exporting their products to other parts of America and to Europe. In his view, the legislation restricted the natural development the American hat industry might otherwise have enjoyed. In this case, confronted with opposing expert interpretations, there is little choice but to examine the arguments more closely. Dickerson's assertion that hatmakers prospered more from a nomadic pursuit of their trade than they would have from fixed industrial locations is not further explained; he presents no specific evidence demonstrating economic advantages enjoyed by wandering hatmakers. Perhaps Harper's argument that the Hat Act was truly a burden to the colonial economy is closer to historical truth.

Finally, restrictions were placed on the colonial iron industry which, like the woolens and hat regulations, had their origins among English interests who looked to Parliament for protection against competition. We know more about this particular phase of British regulation than others because of the studies by Arthur C. Bining, especially those reported in *The*

British Regulation of the Colonial Iron Industry (1933). Bining traced with care the divergent English forces (two basic groups) interested in regulating the colonial iron industry. On one side, the British producers of raw iron (pig and bar iron) were worried about competing with American producers of raw iron and wanted protection against them. On the other side, the users of raw iron, who fabricated it into finished products, were interested in developing sources of raw iron in America but, at the same time, wanted protection against American finished ironwares. Other indirectly related interests were also involved. The owners of wood lots in England, the coal producers, and others whose business connections with one or both sides of the British iron industry would be affected by regulatory legislation, became allies of the antagonists in the battle.

The struggle between British iron interests for protection eventually resulted in the Iron Act of 1750, a victory for the manufacturers of finished ironwares. The legislation encouraged American exportation of pig and bar iron to Britain by eliminating import duties at the port of London (and all British ports after 1757). But new slitting mills, rolling mills, tilt-hammer forges, and steelworks were not to be erected in the provinces. The colonies would produce raw goods, not finished products.

Having traced the complicated origins of the Iron Act, Bining examined the effects of the legislation in the colonies and found that the regulations actually had little direct influence on the development of the American iron industry. No colonial iron works were reported to have been destroyed because of the Parliamentary injunction against finishing mills. No colonist ever was prosecuted for evading or violating the restrictions. Perhaps if colonial fabricated iron products had sought a wider market, infringements would have been noticed and prosecuted. But most of the colonial finished iron was used in the immediate vicinity of its production. Unless provincial governors were willing to seek out actively and destroy the illegal operations (and this they did not do), the Iron Act of 1750, like the Molasses Act of 1733, in actual practice was nullified. No matter how rigidly restrictive the statute reads in the law books, it appears to have had little or no direct effect on the development of the colonial iron industry.

Thus the three specific enactments of Parliament to protect British manufacturers from colonial competition—woolens, hats, and finished iron—appear to have been less than successful. Perhaps only in the case of hats was a potential American industry disrupted by legislation. But before concluding that the statutes were of only minor significance in shaping the colonial economy, it should be noted that there were also less direct, more subtle consequences of the British desire to regulate colonial competition. Lawrence A. Harper, for example, has discussed the possibility (it would be difficult to prove in any quantitative sense) that restrictive legislation, such as the Iron Act, effectively discouraged investments of capital in the regulated industries. Curtis Nettels ("British Mercantilism and the Economic Development of the Thirteen Colonies," *The Journal of Economic History* 12 [Spring 1952]) sees significance in other British regulations affecting colonial industry. Britain regulated or proscribed colonial minting of currency, provincial corporations, commercial banks. The details of some of these policies will be discussed later, but it is useful to remember that these general regulations could substantially alter economic opportunities available to the colonists.

Finally, in considering the application of industrial restraints on the American provinces—the effort by Britain to shape the colonies in complementary rather than competitive forms—it is necessary to indicate that in areas other than direct competition, indeed in often only vaguely related endeavors, Britain's suspicious attitude about American industry generated regulation. Lawrence H. Gipson has one example which demonstrates the point. In the first decades of the eighteenth century, the Virginians enacted a statute designed to encourage the development of towns in their province. Upon receipt of the law for review in England, suspicions were raised that, if allowed, it would tend to lessen tobacco production, which the Crown feared, since royal revenues would be affected, and might also encourage manufactures in Virginia. This was a development

Britain did not favor; the law was disallowed by the king in council. The direct consequences of industrial regulation may have had little to do with the actual shaping of the colonial economy, but general British fears of a rising industrial America probably contributed indirectly to many aspects of imperial policy.

THE MONEY SUPPLY

In addition to Parliamentary legislation restricting ocean commerce, encouraging certain colonial pursuits, and regulating some competitive industries, Britain also attempted to control American currency and coinage. Although this aspect of imperial regulation is sometimes ignored in general evaluations of British policy, such controls actually played significant roles in shaping the patterns of American colonial life. Orthodox mercantilists insisted that the colonies be relegated to a properly dependent condition as far as the minting and circulation of coins were concerned; they viewed such restraints as necessary as regulation of commerce or industry. For gold and silver (specie, bullion) were the visible tokens of national wealth to mercantilists; the accumulation of such wealth in the homeland was a central tenet of their thought. As Britain defined the patterns of economic control within her empire, coinage and currency were increasingly restricted.

The policy was built over a period of decades; the pattern assumed a rather consistent course of following each device the Americans initiated to overcome previous restrictions by new limiting regulations. The theoretical objectives might be constant, but the methods adopted to gain those objectives shifted. First, in line with basic mercantilist belief, came a general proscription of the exportation of coins from the homeland to the colonies. While some parts of the empire at times were released from this general rule (the trade to India, for example, required silver exports from Britain), the American colonies were never excepted from the restriction. This meant that English coins did not ordinarily circulate within the American dominions. Then a corollary was added, prohibiting the minting of coins in the provinces. No silver or gold mines had been discovered in British America, and there had been little effort to create a local coinage by operating colonial mints. Except for a brief experiment that Massachusetts pursued with its "pine tree shillings," and a few other such endeavors, colonial mints had not matured. Now none ever would.

Denied the use of either the currency of the realm or of their own minting for the conduct of commerce and trade, the American colonists were forced to employ such expedient substitutes as they could arrange for themselves. They understood that neither their domestic, imperial, nor (when allowed) foreign commerce could fully develop without some medium of exchange. The southern plantation provinces relied on credit arrangements with the British purchasers of their tobacco, rice, and indigo exports in the conduct of their trans-Atlantic trade. The system was unwieldy, placed the American producer in a poor bargaining position, and in time probably contributed to the historic indebtedness of the colonies—but it did work.

The problem faced by the northern colonists was, in comparison, more difficult. They had no staple export on which to build credits in Great Britain, so they were forced to concoct other devices. As indicated earlier, they found trade with the West Indies particularly useful, for from it they could carry away bills of credit on British merchants, or, even more desirable, specie in foreign coins. The Mediterranean markets of southern Europe were used in the same way. The specie or bills of credit obtained in the Indies or Mediterranean ports could be used for the purchase of British goods. Like the southern planters' credit arrangements, although roundabout and risky, the system worked. But the question to be asked, perhaps, is not whether it worked, but rather, how much more advantageous for the growth of the colonial economy alternate solutions might have proved. Had Britain ever relaxed her restrictions on coinage, or perhaps looked favorably on a separate "imperial" coinage for trade purposes, a major handicap to colonial commerce would have been removed.

Internally—that is, within the colonies—other devices were instituted as substitutes for coins. Besides barter and rudimentary neighborhood credit arrangements, the American colonists constantly overvalued foreign coins in an endeavor to attract them to the mainland. Britain's sensitivity to this overvaluation, and her attempts to regulate the practice, indicate the significance of currency control to mercantile theorists. In the plantation provinces, which had created public warehousing for their staple crops, the colonists learned to use warehouse receipts as a local currency. And, in time, all of the mainland colonies experimented with paper money for domestic use. Colonial paper money was fiat money—notes issued by provincial governments, pledged to be redeemed by means of future tax revenues collected by the colony.

Beginning with a Massachusetts issue in 1690, the early paper currencies were based on anticipated revenues, limited in duration to a few years' circulation, and generally not made legal tender. Since the experiments worked quite satisfactorily for some of the colonies, by the end of Queen Anne's War (1713), there was a desire to continue the practice in peacetime. But the public emergency (defense, war) that had justified the issues was gone, and a new method of securing the bills seemed necessary. It was in answer to these conditions that the idea of creating "land banks" drew adherents.

A "land bank" was conceived on the basic premise of using a colony's most obvious resource—land—as security upon which paper money could be issued. The province would lend to landholders its own fiat money. These loans would be retired in a stated number of years by the borrower, whose interest payments on the loan would provide income for operating the provincial government. Land banks promised advantages of circulating needed paper currency and of providing useful credit facilities for farmers, as well as public revenue. But the colonial merchants disliked the scheme, for it reduced their own economic power, insofar as they controlled local credit supplies. On occasion, as in South Carolina in the 1720s and especially in Massachusetts a little later, creditor merchants fought land-bank promoters in particularly impassioned contests. Parliament came to the aid of the beleaguered merchants in 1741, ending all land-bank promotions by extending the "Bubble Act" of 1720 (legislation which had outlawed unauthorized joint-stock companies in Britain) to the American dominions. And further restrictions on colonial currency experiments were forthcoming. The Currency Act of 1751 proscribed land banks and prohibited the New England colonies from making bills of credit (paper money) legal tender.

Whatever may be said about imperial benefits and trans-Atlantic reciprocities in the general functioning of the navigation acts, Britain's monetary policies imposed upon the American provinces must be cited as one phase of imperial regulation which was narrowly conceived and proved a considerable handicap to the conduct of colonial enterprises, both at home and in overseas commerce. The policies instituted to regulate colonial currency, and the effects of those policies, consistently dramatized one of the basic assumptions of the empire: the colonies were dependencies, and as such, on the especially sensitive questions of coinage and currency, their economic development was at best a secondary consideration, inferior in significance to the fundamental, primary objectives of British mercantilism. It would have been most surprising had it been otherwise, yet it is necessary to keep this in mind in evaluating the economic empire. It is also necessary to remember that the colonists themselves were divided in their opinions about paper money and other methods of satisfying the needs created by the imperial restrictions.

A final facet of economic imperialism to be considered is the growth of the American colonies as markets for British goods. The population of the American mainland colonies increased from an estimated 75,000 in 1660 to 1,593,000 in 1760—a genuinely spectacular increase. As that population grew and extended its standard of living, the American market became correspondingly more significant, both in comparison with colonial raw goods exported and in terms of the total trade of Great Britain. The use of the colonies as markets for British goods had been an admitted objective in mercantilist thought since before the first colony was established in the New World. But, in their early years, with small populations and limited purchasing power, the colonies' major attraction had been their value as sources of raw materials. By mid-eighteenth century the situation had changed, although it is doubtful if Britain fully considered that change in fixing imperial policies. George L. Beer would have argued that it did. He believed, for example, that the British decision, at the conclusion of the Great War for Empire, to retain Canada and restore to France the island of Guadalupe, was an indication of recognition of the increasing importance of the American market. But Clarence Ver Steeg, in *The Formative Years, 1607–1763*, asserts that "contemporary letters, pamphlets, instructions, and legislation do not sustain this thesis."

To the extent that British imperial policies failed to recognize the growing importance of the colonies as markets and, instead, continued to concentrate on them as producers of raw goods, imperial policy was out of step with the realities of the economic empire. Yet the general picture of imperial commerce as historians now paint it is a remarkably pleasant landscape. The estimates of the volume of that trade are revealing. Perhaps one-half of the total colonial trade was directly carried on with the mother country. It is estimated that in 1700 direct trade amounted to approximately one-sixth of the total trade of England; by 1770, the colonial trade had doubled and accounted for one-third of the total British trade. Obviously, such increases indicate vitality in the colonial economy and a more significant role for those colonies in the economy of the British Empire.

AN ASSESSMENT

What then may be said in summary about the general effects of Britain's colonial system on the economy of the American colonies? In balance, it appears that the navigation acts were not a major deterrent, restricting the development of the provinces. Significant sectors of the American economy, especially landholding, were not directly regulated. Some specific enterprises—indigo, naval stores, shipbuilding—were enhanced by imperial encouragement. Other, and even larger, enterprises—tobacco and rice—developed within the machinery of imperial control and prospered as a result of the central marketing features of the empire. Some minor variants appear in the pattern: the Hat Act, perhaps, and the Chesapeake fishing industry, which did not enjoy the privileges accorded New England in importing foreign salt directly into America. But most historians consider the general effect of the legislation to have been more beneficial than burdensome to the colonies.

This general conclusion is derived in part from statistical evidence concerning the expansion of American commerce, industry, and agriculture. Other determining factors have been enlisted as evidence of the healthy state of the colonial economy. Professor Dickerson, for example, pointed to the rapid growth of population as one indicator of economic vitality. The population of British North America not only grew spectacularly; it also increased at a much faster rate than did the British population. Some of this growth resulted from early marriages and large families (both useful as evidence of general well-being) and from the continuing, large immigration to the British colonies, an immigration that would never have taken place had the colonies not been economically attractive. The cultural institutions of colonial society—the churches, colleges, libraries, newspapers, and magazines—all indicate to Dickerson a thriving economy upon which colonists could base their social advances. American colonists were well fed, well housed, and enjoyed a considerable variety of the luxuries of life. In fact, in comparison with the Old World and with other parts of the New World, the British colonists enjoyed a high standard of living. They were able to accumulate goods and wealth, to import large numbers of black slaves and white servants. They filled the Tidewater and Piedmont regions and, by the close of the colonial era, were ready to spill westward over the mountains. Such were the colonial benefits, says Dickerson, of the empire.

Not all scholars, it is true, are as enthusiastic as Dickerson about the imperial pattern; many are more willing to spot flaws in the structure and to emphasize specific features of regulation which worked to the colonists' disadvantage. They would temper their enthusiasm by indicating the sometimes narrow, limited view of imperial planners. They would place more emphasis upon genuinely burdensome features of imperial regulation, such as the controls on currency and even upon ineffective yet discriminatory restraints such as the Molasses Act. Or, as Thomas Barrow suggests, they might argue that the "lack of evidence of colonial opposition could . . . well be taken to show that the Navigation System was ineffective prior to 1763." It appears that those aspects of the imperial system which, in theory, would have been most oppressive to the colonists were mitigated by geography, the relegation of colonial problems to a subordinate position in British affairs of state, or bureaucratic inefficiency. This allowed enough room for colonial expansion to keep American unhappiness at a relatively low level.

What happened to the economic empire after 1763 is not within the province of this book. But by that date it is obvious that a relatively mature and profitable economy had developed in the British colonies. And, having tasted the fruits of such a system, the Americans could be expected to defend their standard of living against all threats—real and imaginary—and to work to increase even further the promises of American colonial life.

THREE

Imperial Politics and Warfare

Economic considerations were primarily responsible for the creation of the first British Empire, and throughout its existence theories and plans for economic gain remained matters of great sensitivity to British imperialists. In time, European wars against other nations with American empires brought Britain's colonial areas into strategic consideration, often dramatically straining relations between parent state and the American dominions. Then there was a less sensitive, less dramatic sphere of imperial concern—the more routine, day-to-day political arrangements through which Britain attempted to direct her colonies toward her economic and strategic goals. Upon the contours of the constitutional structure by which Britain governed her overseas empire, and the responsiveness or lack of responsiveness of the colonists to imperial direction, much of the economic and strategic benefit of the empire would depend. Within the colonies, those same constitutional connections, in varying degrees, helped to shape the structure of American politics and society.

There was division between theory and practice in the economic features of the British Empire, and something of the same division existed in constitutional-political imperial affairs. In theory the empire was, or should be, a relatively tidy unit, with a structure capable of analysis and examination. In actuality, the first British Empire, in its administrative features, lacked clarity and precision. Several major elements contributed to this. Historically, the colonies were created before the empire and, partly through design, probably through desire, Britain never established rigid, central controls over her dominions similar to those of Spain and France. During the seventeenth century, and to a lesser extent the years following, the homeland was engaged in reshaping its own constitutional structure, and this contributed to the ill-defined nature of imperial relationships. And throughout the colonial era, responsibility for imperial affairs was shared by various agencies and bureaus of state.

The supremacy of Parliamentary authority was a central tenet of the British constitution as defined by the Whig settlement after the Glorious Revolution. Ineffectual efforts by small groups during the eighteenth century to return to Stuart rule only emphasized the basic commitment to legislative supremacy. Parliament's primacy was evident not only in affairs at home; the constitution extended beyond the shores of Britain to the dominions. Throughout the colonial era, until the crises preceding the American Revolution gave rise to contrary interpretations, there is little evidence to indicate colonial opposition to the "settlement." Americans not only understood it, they supported it. Lawrence H. Gipson has demonstrated that not only did Parliament act in accordance with the theory in its enactment of trade regulations, currency laws, statutes regarding aliens, and other matters; the colonists themselves acknowledged Parliamentary authority. For example, in 1754, in their efforts to redefine colonial-imperial relationships through the Albany Plan of Union, the Americans believed Parliamentary approval would be necessary to implement the plan. Yet against this theory of Parliamentary supremacy stood the time-honored traditions of Crown responsibility for imperial affairs—traditions and practices continued despite the constitutional rearrangements in Britain after 1689. As Stanley Katz explains, in *Newcastle's New York: Anglo-American Politics, 1732–1753* (1968), "Parliament defined the legal structure of mercantilism in the navigation acts, but the actual enforcement of the navigation system was left to royal administrative officers."

Exactly how the officers, commissions, and boards of imperial control governed the empire in the eighteenth century has been exhaustively described by scholars. Charles M. Andrews devoted the fourth volume of his monumental *The Colonial Period of American History* to the topic; his contemporary in exploring American origins within the British Empire, Herbert L. Osgood, added other dimensions in his multivolume *The American Colonies in the Eighteenth Century* (1924). And the first half of the twentieth century saw the production of many specialized studies that described, analyzed, and explained the British instruments of imperial control. Many of them came from the graduate students of Andrews and Osgood. There still remain fruitful areas for historical research, as Dora M. Clark's *The Rise of the British Treasury* (1960) and Thomas Barrow's *Trade and Empire: The British Customs Service in Colonial America* (1967) indicate. And I. K. Steele, in *Politics of Colonial Policy: The Board of Trade in Colonial Administration, 1696–1720* (1968), illustrates how new questions about familiar topics may be raised—in this case, an inquiry into the interplay between British politics on the one hand, and colonial policy and administration on the other. Interconnections between domestic British politics and the colonies is further delineated in most of the essays comprising Alison Gilbert Olson and Richard Maxwell Brown's *Anglo-American Political Relations, 1675–1775*

(1970) and in Olson's *Anglo-American Politics, 1660–1775: The Relationship between Parties in England and Colonial America* (1973).

Besides the Parliament of Great Britain, along with the slowly evolving cabinet system of ministries, the state offices and agencies sharing responsibility for colonial affairs included the Privy Council, the Board of Trade, the Secretary of State for the Southern Department (who exercised the patronage for the colonies except when the president of the Board of Trade claimed it), the Treasury Board, the Commissioners of the Customs, the Admiralty, War, and Audit offices. Ecclesiastical matters concerning the Anglican Church in America fell within the jurisdiction of the Bishop of London. From the provinces, but resident in Britain, came the agents of the individual colonies, delegates to dispense requested information and to "represent" provincial interests. These were the instruments of empire in Britain. Obviously, in the decades stretching from the Glorious Revolution to the American Revolution, such diffuse responsibility for colonial affairs provided room for a host of statesmen, politicians, clerks, and placemen to test their theories and exercise their authority. Surprisingly there was little experimentation; basic patterns remained relatively unchanged.

Of course there was some shifting in objectives and procedures. Imperial administration reflected changes in Great Britain's governing practices, the comings and goings of personnel, economic expansion, population changes, shifts in social theories and pressures. Diplomacy and war brought differing emphases in imperial affairs. But, in overview, these alterations appear less significant than Britain's adherence to the basic theories laid down during the last decades of the seventeenth century, particularly as "formalized" in the decisions of William III after the Glorious Revolution. Those decisions reflected the general theories of imperial administration and, as a result, the presumed nature of American colonial government. The decision to restore the colonies to their status as of 1670 ensured a continuation of the mixed system developed to that time, with some provinces directly regulated by the Crown, others retained by or restored to their proprietors, and, in the case of Rhode

Island, Connecticut, and (in modified form) Massachusetts, reestablishment of their chartered privileges.

Within this mixture of forms, however, a dominant "type" emerged; the "typical" American province in the eighteenth century was a royal colony. If Britain did not achieve her never-completely-forgotten goal of eventual reduction of all colonies to this form, at least the majority of the American provinces were so classified. New Hampshire was returned to that status after the collapse of the Dominion of New England; Massachusetts, partially by terms of her charter of 1691; New York; New Jersey, after the surrender of governing rights by the proprietors in 1702; Maryland, until the Calverts regained their political rights in 1715; Virginia; the two Carolinas, after the purchase of the proprietary in 1729; Georgia, with the surrender of its charter by the trustees in 1752; the West Indian island possessions, since the post-Restoration years; and, to the north, Newfoundland and Nova Scotia, added in the eighteenth century. These were the royal provinces—the "typical" British-American colonies of the old empire.

THE ROYAL GOVERNOR

In the royal provinces, the character, ability, and personality of the Crown-appointed governor was of great significance in shaping the political, economic, and social life of the colony. While we lack a modern, general evaluation of the royal governors, several studies have delineated the careers of individual governors or, in a less direct fashion, analyses of provincial politics have broadened our understanding of the governor's role. John Schutz, in *William Shirley: King's Governor of Massachusetts* (1961), William Abbot, in his study *The Royal Governors of Georgia, 1754–1775* (1959), and Lawrence Leder, in *Robert Livingston and the Politics of Colonial New York, 1664–1728* (to mention only three of many), have added to our knowledge of the royal governors in America and the part they played in the day-to-day operations of the empire.

Leder, in his study of Livingston's New York career, for example, emphasizes the contributions that Robert Hunter, an able royal governor, made toward long-delayed political stability in that province. Abbot credits Georgia's more astute governors with major contributions to that frontier province's advances. Possessed of considerable potential authority, the governor's office often was used in a constructive way to determine the direction of colonial development. The governor was the central force of imperial authority within his province; whatever actual success British designs might have necessarily rested on the royal governors' understanding, as well as their willingness and ability to direct their colonies toward those imperial objectives.

As the chief British officer in a royal province, the governor was the natural center of imperial officialdom, around whom other imperial agents—customs officers, naval officers, surveyors general, attorneys general, receivers general, and others—gravitated. Some sought his advice, some his favor. He was expected to give encouragement and direction, and he might, without great effort, find himself the leader of what some historians have termed the "court party" or "court faction" in provincial politics. His fellow agents in imperial management were naturally attached to his group. Colonists who sought his favors and preferments might also join.

The governor's powers extended beyond administering imperial statutes and orders within his assigned province. By his commission and instructions, he possessed authority bearing directly on the course of provincial political events. He nominated men to the council, the group of royally appointed advisers who, in conjunction with the governor, administered colonial affairs, formed the upper house of colonial legislatures, and sat in judicial capacity as the highest court in most of the provinces. In his joint activities with the council, the governor could direct the course of legislation, land distribution, defense measures, and justice. His powers (at least theoretically) over the elected lower house of assembly, and through that agency into the domestic political life of the province, were also ample. He held an absolute veto over legislation, and the power to summon, adjourn, prorogue, and dissolve the assembly. And, if astute, he could extend his authority into the realm of local government, the county and subcounty levels, where his powers of appointment could be used to reward friends and punish opponents, thereby advancing his designs for the province or his own career.

Thus the governor was, or might become, the central agent both in imperial affairs and domestic activities within his province. If he was a man of limited ability, with narrowly conceived ambitions or views of his province's needs, he might be unable to control factionalism and political strife, and the province and his own reputation suffered. Lawrence Leder has shown the results of a series of such New York governors. On the other hand, an able, determined governor such as Robert Hunter of New York, as described by Leder, or Governors Ellis and Wright of Georgia, as seen by Abbot, or Massachusetts's Governor Shirley, as portrayed by John Schutz, could advance both the province's and his own interests, stabilizing political activities, working diligently to accentuate programs of compatible interest to colony and empire, and effectively reducing the areas of contention between homeland and America.

In many respects, the governor's life was not enviable. He might, at times, be like the proverbial servant with two masters, capable of satisfying neither. Not only did he have to build a position of strength domestically within the province and to identify himself as being at least concerned about, if not always wholly committed to, local ambitions and aspirations; he was also dependent for continuance in office upon men and interests in the homeland which often—perhaps usually—had little concern for imperial designs. In the flexible, shifting political world of eighteenth-century Britain, a governor achieved office because of his relationships with those in power, not because of his administrative abilities; his continuation in office depended upon his talents in retaining a base of support back home.

Despite this, he needed also to consider the instructions he received from the official agencies in England charged with administration of colonial affairs—the Board of Trade, the Treasury, the Customs Commissioners. Beset then with theoretical objectives and practical considerations on both sides of the Atlantic, the governor was unlikely to satisfy all the demands upon him. Perhaps the most significant conclusion from a survey of the careers of those men who held the office during the eighteenth century is not their failure to advance imperial designs, but rather their ability to accommodate, to the extent that they did, the imperial needs with local interests and desires. In fact, recent explanations of Anglo-American political interrelationships help us understand how some governors survived and, at times, carved successful careers. Stanley Katz observes that "the tone of American politics . . . was set by a natural interaction of English and American politics"; ". . . the ministry and the Americans, do not appear irreconcilable, and the true challenge [to governors] was to master them both rather than to skirt their mysterious dangers."

If, until after 1763, the American colonists entertained no serious thoughts about "independence" or life outside the imperial orbit—and historians seem agreed that this was true—then the royal governors, the central agents bridging Britain and her colonies, proved sufficiently flexible, useful agents in accommodating differences, allowing scope for satisfactory expression of both imperial and colonial aspirations. How much "accident" and how much "design" were involved in this situation is difficult to determine. As indicated earlier, Britain never proceeded in her imperial plans from assumptions of control structured along such rigid lines as Spanish or French imperial regimentation. British colonial governors were expected to dominate and direct colonial administration, not to monopolize it. Yet even with these moderate "theoretical" powers assigned to the governors, it was probably more accident than design that led to the erosion of authority from the office, providing increasing opportunities for colonial participation in government.

Distance from the seat of empire, and the slowness of eighteenth-century communication, contributed to the separation between theory and practice. So did the diffusion of responsibility for colonial affairs among various agencies within the British government. James A. Henretta in *"Salutary Neglect": Colonial Administration under the Duke of Newcastle* (1972) explains: "Over the years, the governors lost their ability to manage the colonial assemblies in the interest of the home government. In the last analysis, this loss of power stemmed from the growing divergence between the social, economic, and political interests of the American colonies and those of the mother country. But this inevitable development was accelerated by the neglect of colonial problems by those in London and by the shortsighted and selfish patronage policies pursued by politicians. . . ." And Bernard Bailyn, in *Origins of American Politics* (1968), identifies structural flaws in the governor's office, particularly the lack of real patronage leverage, that explain the erosion of executive authority and a consequent loss of stability in colonial politics.

It is a fact that, until very late in the colonial era, no royal governor was removed from office because he disobeyed instructions. Warfare with France and Spain, and its attendant crises in America, created moments of emergency when rules could be ignored for immediate needs, thus setting precedents that were continued in peacetime. The results of all this can be seen in the American attitudes toward royal governors. Some were loved, a few were detested, but the office was rarely damned as an engine of perpetual tyranny. The longer the colonists lived with the system, the more they learned to turn its weaknesses to their advantage.

From a twentieth-century "managerial" viewpoint, with its emphasis on efficient administration, eighteenth-century royal governorships left much to be desired. At any given moment, chaotic conditions would seem to have been the rule. But, in the larger sense of historical development, the royal governors evidently served as useful "shock absorbers," cushioning collisions between local and imperial ambitions. That cushioning effect, however, played to the ultimate advantage of the colonies, for they gradually assumed ever greater control over their own development. In filling the vacuums of power created before 1763, they built precedents and established procedures of local control that one day would prove disastrous for the empire.

THE LOWER HOUSES OF ASSEMBLY

The theory of the empire fixed the royal governor as the central agency of colonial government. In actual practice, however, by the close of the colonial era the elected lower houses of assembly had come to more than a position of parity in power with the governors—they had eclipsed them as the principal instruments of governmental power within the provinces. The rise of the colonial assemblies and the contests for power waged with royal governors have long been staple ingredients in the historian's narrative of colonial development. New details of that story have been explained by Jack P. Greene in *The Quest for Power: The Lower Houses of Assembly in the Southern Royal Colonies, 1689–1776* (1963). While the corresponding history of the lower houses in the middle and northern provinces needs similar study, there is probably much in Greene's findings that is applicable throughout the American colonial experience.

The story, again, is one of division between theory and practice, between the ideal of empire as envisioned by British theorists on the one hand and the actual functioning government in America on the other. It constitutes as significant a pattern in the history of political development as in the economic history of the empire. Theory and ideals pointed toward a unified, consolidated imperial structure, with Crown, Parliament, and colonial administrators linked in logical arrangements for governing the overseas dominions. Over and against the theory was the actual developing practice of government in the colonies, affording opportunities for the lower houses of assembly, elected by and responsive to the wishes of the colonists, to reach out and attain even greater measures of control.

Historians have long pointed to the control of colonial revenues as the primary mechanism by which the lower houses of assembly gained power at the expense of royal governors. The "power of the purse" has been pictured as the weapon of control in the colonies, in rough similarity to Parliament's financial regulation of the declining royal power at home. The governors, caught between colonial and imperial forces, were brought to surrender by the Americans' insistence on their right to regulate public finances, including the sensitive matter of governors' salaries. Greene, however, has shown that this simplified explanation of the shifting center of governing control is too rudimentary to describe the actual situation in the southern provinces. He demonstrates, in fact, both the complexities of the shift, which extended into a vast number of areas and concerns, and the fact that the matter of the governors' salaries, far from being the only, or even the major, method of gaining ascendancy over the royal executives, was not a major controversy in the southern provinces. For there, in most cases, the governors were provided with annual salaries from sources beyond the reach of the local assemblies.

The development of legislative control, according to Greene, was a much more complex story, developing along various "fronts" and bringing a mixture of successes and failures to the colonists as they sought power for their lower houses of assembly. Public finance was one of the major areas in which the lower houses satisfied that quest, but in a more extensive manner than merely manipulating governors' salaries. The southern provinces used the power to tax as a springboard from which they eventually claimed the right to frame general supervisory control over finances of a public nature, including the right to audit accounts of public officers, appoint and maintain public treasurers, order the dispersal of public funds, and (although circumscribed by imperial restrictions) engage in emission of paper money. And, while the governors' salaries were not within the regulating range of the lower houses, the fees and thus the fortunes accruing to the executive were, and the control of fees, added to the increasing list of other methods of regulating financial affairs, gave to the lower houses of assembly the primary position in colonial money matters. This position, once gained, could be used as a lever for securing authority in other governmental concerns.

Control of raising and dispersing public moneys, for example, could be used as an instrument to manage public services, such as public printing, with its corresponding regulatory authority over public information, as well as the agency, or "representation" of colonial affairs in London, military matters, Indian affairs, judicial concerns, and even ecclesiastical affairs. The penetration of assembly influence into these areas of government certainly was not uniformly successful, nor did it occur simultaneously in all of the southern provinces. But what Greene has discerned as immensely significant is that, in their quest for power, the lower houses of assembly in the plantation provinces moved to establish themselves as a part of the decision-making, policy-setting machinery in all areas. And all of the southern houses had achieved some measure of success by 1763.

There were directions where the drive for legislative power made little or no headway, and even directions where power once exercised by colonial assemblymen was regained by imperial authorities. Greene identifies the movement to control the "composition and proceedings" of the lower houses them-selves as one segment of the contest in which some of the most significant colonial aspirations were never realized. The model used by the colonial assemblies in their quest was the pattern of the House of Commons of Great Britain. The American colonists consciously viewed their local assemblies as miniature replicas of the Commons; they sought duplication of privileges and immunities enjoyed by members of Parliament for their local legislators. In some areas they succeeded, winning recognition of members' freedom in speech, in debate, and from arrest, as well as the right to settle disputed elections and to choose the speaker of the lower house. But in other, quite significant matters, their drive was frustrated; for example, they never completely gained their desired control of scheduling elections or sessions. Representation, or apportionment, was controlled through the device of creating new counties, often by dividing established ones. In these matters the colonists made little progress against the Crown's determination to retain control.

But, in Greene's view, these setbacks were of less signif-icance than the gains the colonists made. If they did not achieve absolute victory in their reach for power, they did succeed in effecting sufficient changes to alter the basic constitutional arrangements of the empire. By 1763, the center of power in the colonies was no longer in the royal governor and his agencies of control, but rather in the lower houses of assembly. And herein was a real division between theory and practice. For the Americans were living within an imperial structure that operated quite differently from the structure Britain believed to be outlined by her constitutional arrangements. "From Edward Randolph in the last decades of the seventeenth century to the . . . 1750s," Greene concludes, "colonial officials had envisioned a highly centralized empire with a uniform political system in each of the colonies and with the imperial government closely supervising the subordinate governments. But because they had never made any sustained or systematic attempt to achieve these goals during the first half of the eighteenth century, there had developed a working arrangement permitting the lower houses considerable latitude in shaping colonial constitutions without requiring Crown or Proprietary officials to give up any of their ideals. That there had been a growing divergence between imperial theory and colonial practice mattered little so long as each refrained from openly challenging the other." One day, of course, the challenges would come, but that day was still in the future.

COLONISTS AND GOVERNMENT

There was another level of government in the British North American colonies, below the imperial agencies and the provincial institutions, which perhaps most directly affected the average colonist. The ordinary citizen, concerned with the daily routine of getting and spending—sheltering and feeding and defending himself and his family—probably was aware of imperial actions, or even colonial legislators, only during extraordinary moments. Colonists dealt most directly with their county or town government, which had been developed in answer to the needs of the local communities. These county or town governments have been termed the most stable agencies of government in colonial America. Wesley Frank Craven, in his study of *The Southern Colonies in the Seventeenth Century*, has pointed to the need for more fully appreciating the role local governments played in colonial development; Clarence Ver Steeg, in *The Formative Years, 1607–1763*, endorses the theme: "Rebellions might come and go, but local government provided an anchor that enabled the colonials to weather the storm. Indeed, the fact that local government in America has survived a revolution, a civil war, an industrial revolution, and global responsibilities is one of the most impressive yet most neglected aspects in the history of American political institutions." Ver Steeg suggests that, in addition to their vitality and usefulness, local governments also provided a basically divisive force within the colonial world. In England, local government was administered directly through agencies related to the national government and thus furnished a vehicle for furthering a "vertical-type" nationalism. Conversely, in the colonies, local government tended to operate in a manner that discouraged centralization and uniformity.

It is, perhaps, easier to see this result in the New England region than in the southern provinces. The New England town meetings afforded convenient and presumably democratic methods for conducting local public affairs. The freemen of a town could participate directly in fashioning policies for the community, generally divorced from influence or pressures from provincial or imperial interests. In the southern provinces, county governments were the primary agencies of local administration, and theoretically, imperial influences might be exerted there through the royal governor's appointive power in the offices of the justice of the peace. The justices were the chief local administrators, combining supervision of local public affairs with their judicial duties. Since they were appointed by the governor, rather than elected, and since they might also be in the governor's debt for commissions as local militia officers or other favors, they were theoretically less free as agents than the town officers in New England. Yet, in many cases, the governor's powers had been closely circumscribed by methods of nomination, and in the southern as well as the northern colonies, local administrators exercised their powers relatively free from imperial regulation.

Their duties were such that their offices rarely became

arenas of contest between local and imperial interests; their function, and their virtue, resulted from their attention to the routine needs of their immediate communities. Whether northern or southern, town or county, the officers of local administration supervised the construction, maintenance, and operation of roads, bridges, and ferries. They looked after welfare needs of orphans, widows, and indigents. They organized and supplied the militia units. They worried about broken fences and stray cattle. They set tax levies and collected revenue, licensed grogshops and taverns, and dispensed justice in minor litigation. The ordinary settler paid his taxes to this government, looked to it for protection, and resorted to its courts when he sought justice. By its stability in times of crisis, its familiarity as a permanent fixture of his immediate world—like church, chapel, or burying ground—it represented law, order, and authority in the settler's known world. Provincial government and provincial politics were removed and distant, perhaps several days' travel away. As for imperial administration and the affairs of the empire, they were even more remote and of less concern.

This "layered" arrangement—extending from the British Crown and Parliament through royal officials resident in the colonies to colonial assemblies and down to local units of administration, town and county governments—provided the framework within which colonial political life operated. It was always, everywhere, a richly varied structure. Within it could be found places of honor and places of fortune, offices appointive and offices elective, elements of aristocracy and elements of democracy. Lacking precision and uniformity, it seems almost to defy general description. Yet historians continue to ask the question, and seek its answer: What was the nature of the political life, and the society shaping and shaped by the politics of provincial America? Was the overall tone of colonial life aristocratic, structured by institutions and inclinations into stratified classes assuring political, social, and economic privileges to the few? Or was colonial life democratic, exhibiting unusual (for its, or perhaps any, age) opportunities for individual satisfaction in political, social, and economic aspirations?

These questions have engendered more debate than most

interpretive problems concerning colonial America. Much of the interest originates in attempts to assess the nature of the American Revolution, which lead, in turn, to analyses of the structure of pre-Revolutionary provincial politics and society. The "case" for a democratic interpretation of colonial life, with particular emphasis on political democracy, has been argued by Robert E. Brown in *Middle-Class Democracy and the Revolution in Massachusetts, 1691–1780* (1955), and in a second study, written with B. Katherine Brown, *Virginia, 1705–1786: Democracy or Aristocracy?* (1964). In seeking answers, the Browns have relied on two major types of evidence—statistical analyses of voting records and population characteristics, and indications of contemporary opinions regarding the nature of political and social structures from the literary remains of the eighteenth century. The conclusions they reach are generally unqualified assertions of provincial democracy in both Massachusetts and Virginia.

The statistical analyses of suffrage in the colonies presented in these studies seem more convincing than the expressions of contemporary opinion concerning democratic or aristocratic tendencies. The Massachusetts characterizations, in particular, too often are drawn from statements of British officials attempting to explain failure or frustration of their administrations on the basis of "excessive" colonial democracy. Although some critics have questioned the statistical methods employed, historians generally have been more interested in, and probably more persuaded by, the Browns' assertions concerning voting privileges and restrictions. They have found that the suffrage regulations laid down for election of members of the lower houses of assembly were much less restrictive than formerly had been supposed. In both Massachusetts and Virginia, property qualifications were easily met by the majority of adult white male colonists. The Browns emphasize who *could* vote, not who *did* vote, for it appears that the suffrage, although widely distributed among the Virginia and Massachusetts colonists, was less widely exercised.

These assertions of colonial American democracy converted some scholars, but not all, and the controversy continues.

Critics have raised valid queries. Merrill Jensen, for example, in "Democracy and the American Revolution," *Huntington Library Quarterly* 20 (August 1957), asserts that ". . . colonial governments on the eve of the Revolution did not function democratically, nor did the men who controlled them believe in democracy. Even if we agree that there was virtually manhood suffrage, in Massachusetts, it is difficult . . . to see it as a democracy. In 1760 the government was controlled by a superb political machine headed by Thomas Hutchinson, who with his relatives and political allies occupied nearly every important political office in the colony except the governorship. The Hutchinson oligarchy controlled the superior court, the council, the county courts, and the justices of the peace; with this structure of appointive office spread throughout the colony, it was able to control the house of representatives elected by the towns . . . if Massachusetts had a democratic leader, that man was Thomas Hutchinson, a charge to which he would have been the first to issue a horrified denial."

As for the governorship, which Hutchinson did not control, that office was filled by Crown appointment. And in Virginia, an even larger proportion of provincial officers were appointed, not elected. The Browns, in their study of Virginia, seem to concede something of the argument in a brief but significant section of their analysis, indicating that the colonial voters there enjoyed a direct voice only in the selection of members of the House of Burgesses. All other Virginia offices were filled by appointment. The conditions and procedures by which candidates announced or were chosen for office also need more study. How fully were all interests in colonial society represented in the slate of candidates? What barriers, if any, disqualified some men from consideration and what encouragements, if any, propelled others toward public service?

Interesting as the question of democracy, or its limitations, in colonial America is, it need not have concerned us in this general review of colonial-imperial relationships except for one fact: The Browns have interpreted American opposition to British imperial regulation largely in terms of a dichotomy between aristocracy and democracy. The British Empire, or at least its agents, in their view, was aristocratic; the American colonies were democratic. As Robert Brown has stated in a review, colonial democracy and British imperialism were "two essentially incompatible forces"; it was democracy in the colonies which kept the mercantile system from being effectively enforced and threatened independence from imperial rule. In *Middle-Class Democracy and the Revolution in Massachusetts,* Brown explains that ". . . in all this, there was no hint of a controlling aristocracy . . . opposed to a disfranchised and underprivileged class; in fact, the British would have been much happier than they were if such an aristocracy existed. What was needed was some way to curtail the over-abundance of demo-cratic customs which already existed, so that Britain could enforce her mercantile system and secure the dependence of the colonies on the mother country."

This reading of the history of imperial relationships tends to polarize imperial-provincial interests, connoting monomorphic political and social conditions in the colonies and in imperial agencies. It leaves little room for the more subtle identification of interest groupings which other historians have described as characteristic of provincial society—groups which, in the fluidity of colonial social structures, ordinarily divided between an older, more mature elite, enjoying social, economic, and political power, and a newer, rising group, perhaps already in possession of economic power and anxious to gain corresponding social and political privileges. In the Browns' view, there was no real American aristocracy; in the opposing view, there were both aristocrats and would-be aristocrats willing to align themselves with or against imperial agencies according to their estimates of how such alignment might help or hinder their own welfare. In one view, the friction was always between colonies and empire; in the other, friction could be generated as easily by internal struggles as by imperial relationships. In fact, as long as colonial opportunities for individual advancement existed and colonial society remained fluid, such frictions were very likely to develop.

A further difference in interpretation results from the assertion by Robert Brown that the frictions between the colonies and the empire were constant features of imperial politics. He has labeled the state of the empire as one of "perpetual discordance," filled with inevitable clashes between the democratic, colonial way of life and an aristocratic British philosophy. Other scholars, impressed with the beneficial effects of imperial relationships, have characterized the normal state of the empire as harmonious, with the occasional eruption of discordance the exception, not the rule. Between these two characterizations—discordance and harmony—there seems little room for a composite assessment.

Whatever the "normal" state of imperial relationships (and no final statement would satisfy all historians), international warfare and its accompanying dislocations brought crises in understanding between parent state and provinces. Imperial defense and aggressive warfare against neighboring empires placed unusual strains on British-colonial relations, exposing otherwise half-hidden cleavages between them.

THE EMPIRE IN WAR

The basic motivation for forging an English empire in the years from 1660 to 1690 had been economic. American colonies, regulated in England's interest, would increase the trade of English merchants, generate revenues for the Crown, and produce profits from landholding for proprietary lords and gentlemen. These economic considerations, and the means to further them, led to policies establishing political controls and clarifying constitutional relationships between colonies and mother country. After 1689, while economic impulses continued to influence imperial statecraft, the basic motivating forces propelling attempts to unify and strengthen imperial controls probably stemmed from strategic and military considerations. Beginning in 1689 with the War of the League of Augsburg (King William's War, in America), Britain would wage a series of conflicts against France and her allies—the War of the Spanish Succession (Queen Anne's War), the War of Jenkin's Ear against Spain, which merged into the more comprehensive War of the Austrian Succession (King George's War), and the final conflict, the Great War for Empire (French and Indian

War, Seven Years' War) ending in 1763. Each of these conflicts led Britain to consider her American provinces in a manner different from older, earlier concepts.

Theoretical strategic arguments for creation and maintenance of an overseas empire had been part of the rationale for imperial endeavors from the beginning. But not until after 1689 were such theories actually put to major tests. Then the potential strategic and military advantages and disadvantages of overseas possessions became sensitive considerations in shaping policies for the empire. Klaus Knorr, in his analysis of *British Colonial Theories, 1570–1850* (1944), identified four separate arguments stressing strategic advantages British theorists and publicists claimed would accrue from possession of overseas territories. Each of them contributed in some measure to the overall impulse for empire building.

The first assertion stressed the advantage overseas colonies would bring Britain in attacking the colonies of enemy nations or harassing the trade of enemy empires. During the sixteenth and early seventeenth centuries, such thought presumably was directed against Spain: British colonies in America would offer convenient bases for hostile raids on Spanish possessions and commerce. Secondly, in a more general fashion, overseas colonies would bring Britain increased mastery of the seas. A third advantage was the function colonies might play in the homeland's constant concern to maintain security through a "balance of power" among European nations, some of which were also building non-European empires. If other nations— Spain, France, Holland—became too powerful because of their Asian, African, or American colonies, Britain would need colonies of her own to restore an equilibrium. Finally, arguing a defensive role for overseas possessions, it was suggested that new or expanded colonial possessions might be required to safeguard valuable British colonies already in existence. This last assumed a continuing commitment in empire building; in contests for empire, the homeland might be forced to establish defensive colonies to protect mature possessions from hostile rivals.

Thus, at least in theory, colonies were strategically, militarily useful to the mother country, capable of offering both defensive and offensive benefits in the nation's trade rivalries, diplomacy, and warfare against enemy states. In the eighteenth century the British people would be given an opportunity to test these theories from an earlier era and to discover that, along with the strategic benefits colonies offered, there was also a price to be paid. The "price of empire" turned out to be the cost of defending it, for an increasingly large expenditure in troops and money was required to safeguard already established British dominions. Ultimately even the last of the early theories proved true, for European powers eventually sought to balance their world by waging warfare in America.

There had been a time in the earlier years of European expansion and colony building when the overseas possessions were considered a separate sphere, divorced from the wars of European statecraft. The concept of there being "no peace beyond the line" of demarcation had created two worlds, and the American world was not part of the European world as far as conventional diplomacy and warfare were concerned. What this meant was that Europeans could raid, plunder, and even capture New World settlements of other nations without such activities interfering with the regular relationships between those powers in Europe.

Perhaps partly because the rules of the game separated warfare in Old and New Worlds, and perhaps also because it coincided with the basic royal policy of extending no direct financial subsidy for discovery or colonization, the English theory of imperial defense was rooted in the belief that the American colonists could, would, and should protect themselves. John Shy has reviewed that theory in the introductory chapter of *Toward Lexington: The Role of the British Army in the Coming of the American Revolution* (1965). Shy explains the underlying ideas of imperial defense—basic dependence on colonial militia units, locally raised, equipped, and officered—and then he fills out the story by demonstrating that the theory, like so many imperial theories, often was ignored in the exigencies of the actual occasion. Britain did commit military forces and naval power to the defense of the American empire. Fictitious though the theory may have become, it was not renounced until 1754 when, after a century and a half of allegiance to the older view, Britain reversed her assumptions to square more closely with the realities of the empire. At the start of the Great War for Empire, Britain decided to commit men and money in major proportions in order to defeat France, not in Europe, but in America. The alternative would have been to allow France to win the Ohio Valley, something neither the British nor the American colonists desired.

In the evolving partnership in warfare that linked Britain and her American colonies during the years 1689 to 1763, there was ample time for ideas to develop or be modified. Lessons learned in early conflicts might be remembered during later events, and ideas dimly perceived at the beginning of the eighteenth century might well have become strong convictions by 1755. The military partnership almost inevitably generated misunderstandings and grievances that marred imperial harmony. If, given the modern instruments for communication and control that twentieth-century military men are able to command, partners in alliances still argue about goals and procedures, how much more reasonable to expect that British imperial relationships would have felt strains during attempts at cooperatively waging war.

Even an unadorned list of imperial misunderstandings, jealousies, quarrels, and grievances would fill the pages of a book; a few examples must suffice to illustrate the nature of the problem. During Queen Anne's War, in 1709, after plans had been laid for a joint assault on French Canada, Britain decided not to commit the force she had agreed to furnish and delayed for several months notifying the colonists of her decision. George M. Waller, in his biography *Samuel Vetch: Colonial Enterpriser* (1960), comments that "it was only good sense" for the ministry in England to defer British forces from joining the Americans, since peacemaking was under way in Europe and it appeared that captured colonies would be restored to their previous owners if the negotiations were successful. But, Waller adds, while this exonerates the British in the decision, at the time the reasons for the abrupt change were not known to the Americans, and thus were of no aid in alleviating their unhappiness. What made the situation even worse was that the colonists, for once, had really exerted themselves to prepare for the combined attack. And the cavalier attitude of the British, in their failure to inform the Americans of their decision in time to halt preparation in the colonies, indicated a lack of consideration that could only aggrieve the colonists who were trying to cooperate in a common venture.

Trevor R. Reese, in *Colonial Georgia: A Study of British Imperial Policy in the Eighteenth Century* (1963), similarly assesses an incident of 1740, when a planned attack on St. Augustine in Spanish Florida failed because of insufficient support from Britain. Reese shows that however significant the capture of the place might have appeared to the Georgians, in the larger strategy of the war a minor objective like St. Augustine should not have been allowed to divert energies or attention from more significant objectives on the Continent or elsewhere in the Western Hemisphere. And similar episodes could be repeated. The return to France of the fortress at Louisbourg on Cape Breton Island, captured by the Americans during King George's War and returned as part of the peace settlement, insulted the colonists' pride. Nor were the lack of strategic planning, poor communications, inefficient procedures, or indifferent attitudes the only causes for American bitterness toward Britain in wartime. Matters of military rank between colonial units and regular British army forces, the quotas requested in soldiers and supplies, impressment or attempts at impressment of colonists into the Royal Navy, and other issues provoked animosity and sometimes even led to rioting.

There were, of course, corresponding frustrations experienced by Britain. Colonial responses to requests for joint ventures often seemed lethargic, halfhearted; continued pleas for unified action brought no improvement in the chaotic patterns of the colonies toward war measures; the quality of the colonial militiaman as a fighting soldier—these and many more incidents and situations form the other part of the story. The historian who attempts to analyze actions must carefully examine the evidence remaining from those times, remembering that it is far easier for the scholar of today to understand and appreciate British policy decisions and actions than it was for eighteenth-century American colonists, who lacked the information and perhaps the perspective to view the conflicts in their overall dangers and opportunities.

THE COLONIES AND WAR

In reviewing the history of *The Colonial Wars: 1689–1762* (1964), Howard H. Peckham has illustrated how events during the first of those conflicts, King William's War, demonstrated flaws in imperial theories regarding responsibility for defense of the empire. England had committed herself in America in only a limited fashion in that war. She had dispatched only four companies of soldiers to America, relying upon the colonists to devise their own defense and whatever offensive operations they might arrange against the French. The result, in Peckham's view, was that the colonists learned an awareness of the need to provide for their own defense, an awareness that might have been reluctantly accepted, but nonetheless became a part of colonial thought. On the other hand, on the basis of the colonists' record, the British concluded that the colonies could easily marshal the necessary men and equipment both to defend themselves and to conquer French Canada, if only they would stop bickering amongst themselves and forget their fears about the royal prerogative. These concepts, says Peckham, as vehicles for misunderstanding, would continue to mar harmonious imperial relationships until the Peace of Paris in 1763.

Peckham also sees concepts of mutual interest developing during the early warfare. For example, he believes that, in the northern provinces, the belief that frontier security could be permanently maintained only by pushing the French off the continent took root and, while slowly nurtured, ". . . in two generations this tantalizing hope would mature to a widespread and passionate conviction . . ." among Americans. And the first experience in imperial warfare demonstrated to the colonists the benefits from intercolonial cooperation, for ". . . although the joint military effort had failed, at least there had been official discussions. The participants were dimly aware that they had certain common problems, such as defense, and that the burden of the solutions might be lightened by some sort of joint action."

These statements by Peckham introduce these topics of interest to historians—the ability (or willingness) of the Americans to provide for their own defense; the attitude of the Americans toward the imperial conflicts; and the impetus that military matters brought to the problems of intercolonial cooperation and possible union.

Daniel Boorstin, in the concluding sections of his provocative book, *The Americans: The Colonial Experience* (1958), comments on the willingness of the colonists to enter into the imperial conflicts. He characterizes the performance of Americans during the Great War for Empire as one of generally limited and grudging contributions. He sees the British burden proportionately greater than that of the colonists, and explains the reluctance of Americans to cooperate fully in the war partly as a result of their long-endured necessity to provide for their own defense against Indian threats. Life in wilderness America, explains Boorstin, required the maintenance and exercise of arms on an individual (family) basis. Accustomed to that state of personal defense, the colonist believed that local (community) defense was a necessity and contributed to it for his own personal protection. But warfare of an offensive nature, against colonial possessions of Spain or France, involved other theories and other practices. It required deployment of men outside provincial boundaries, leaving the "homeland" of the colonist open and undefended. This led to a serious hesitation in providing requested men and supplies and to the failure of colonies to cooperate with each other in wartime.

Moreover, even when commitments were forthcoming, Boorstin believes that the American colonist made a rather dismal showing as a soldier, citing the 1754 capture of Louisbourg as the only instance of a successful, provincial, large-scale military operation. He ascribes that victory to "lucky coincidence" rather than applied strategy. Boorstin asserts that colonial troops were ill-trained, lacking in order and neatness, undisciplined, and living a "free and easy" life under the command of elected officers. They could not be counted on in actual battle, and in the end military victories against France and Spain were possible only when Britain fielded a professional army in America.

Not only did the American colonists follow their own ideas about military defense; they were also reluctant to engage in warfare as a result of their lack of interest in conquest for expansion of the empire, according to Boorstin. He further asserts that the ordinary provincial Americans, be they either western pioneers concerned with their own protection against the "local" danger, or the more secure American colonists on the seaboard, were not moved by concepts of expanding empires or opening new areas for British control or reducing French control in Canada. They were, says Boorstin, much more interested in keeping the New World out of European power politics. In effect, Americans were already isolationists.

Boorstin's characterization of Americans as uninterested in European diplomacy, desirous of pursuing parochial, isolated interests, is challenged by other scholars. Howard H. Peckham, as indicated above, argues the opposite was true, claiming that the Americans came to accept the doctrine that the elimination of the French from North America was essential to their security. Max Savelle and Darold D. Wax (*A History of Colonial America*, 1973) contend that, rather than being "pawns" of European diplomacy, the colonists were as anxious for wars of expansion as their British cousins, for the Americans, no less than the British, equated war with empire, and "empire meant profit."

Lawrence H. Gipson, who has studied the events of the Great War for Empire in more detail than any other scholar, in the sixth volume of *The British Empire before the American Revolution*, explains why historians have misunderstood the colonists' reactions to the imperial struggles. Gipson believes that historians too often view the events of those years through the eyes of propagandists for the American Revolution, particularly through the writings of Thomas Paine. In his *Common Sense* Paine painted a picture of independence guaranteeing an isolated, secure America, free from the danger of being "dragged into" unnecessary and unwanted warfare by Britain. To make the dream purer, Paine suggested that the colonists never really had any interest in the warfare of the last three-quarters of a century; they had become engulfed in those wars only because they were a part of the British Empire. But it was Englishmen who had reaped the advantages, said Paine, leaving the colonists to pay a disproportionate share in money, material, and human lives.

Gipson believes that Paine has misled historians such as George Bancroft and others into a wrong assessment of the colonists' role in the struggle for empire in North America. He questions ". . . whether any responsible American in any of the colonies could have been found during the years between 1750 and 1760 who would have subscribed to Paine's beliefs." Gipson cites requests from the colonists for military aid; he asserts that it was France, not England, who began the troubles by sending an armed force into the Ohio Valley. Once begun, the war was continued by colonists who quickly looked to England for aid in winning the western area. Britain then faced a choice: it could pursue a narrow policy, calculate the cost of trading losses as the Dutch presumably had done in the seventeenth century, and if the colonies were not worth rescuing, could have refused aid; or, rejecting this, Britain could, and did, make a decision on the basis of newer, eighteenth-century concepts of colonialism—concepts that involved full protection and security for all parts of the empire.

The decision made, Britain proceeded to fight for retention of the Ohio Valley, turning the North American theater (especially under the energetic and capable leadership of William Pitt) into the principal arena of the entire conflict. The victory of British arms on the Plains of Abraham above Quebec City in 1759 is counted as one of the decisive battles of the modern world, for it sealed the future of the French American empire and marked the high point of Britain's quest for mastery over her long-time rival. That war also brought significant internal changes to Britain's overseas empire: it provided the occasion for serious consideration of the need for intercolonial cooperation and led to the appointment of a supreme commander of forces in North America for the first time in the history of the empire.

Military matters were not the only elements contributing to ideas for imperial unification in the mid-eighteenth century. The earlier imperialists' concern with uniformity had never been completely forgotten, and from time to time suggestions for consolidating controls in the interests of improving the Indian trade or commercial and industrial regulations were made. But, in the eighteenth century, military problems were most often responsible for reviving possibilities of intercolonial union.

Some minor modifications had been instituted. For example, the royal governors of New York and Massachusetts had been given military supervision over the neighboring corporate colonies of Connecticut and Rhode Island. But larger plans were never carried to fruition. In 1721, motivated by experiences in the early wars, the Board of Trade put together a blueprint for unified control, calling for the appointment of an officer who would serve as the king's principal agent in America. His authority would allow him to coordinate colonial military efforts in raising men and money. But the plan had never been effected; no such officer had been appointed.

In 1754, on the eve of the Great War for Empire, the Board of Trade returned to the issue of consolidating control in the colonies, proceeding to frame a plan of union. And the threat of that war led to the summoning of the Albany Conference in America, to consider Indian, defense, and military problems and possibilities of greater colonial cooperation. The Albany Conference, of course, went far beyond the immediate war threat in drafting a plan of union, offering a scheme that would have erected a general, dominionlike status for the American provinces. That plan proved unacceptable to both Britain and to the individual colonies in America. The Board of Trade's scheme never became more than a "paper plan."

Nonetheless, when war broke out and the British decided to field an army in the New World, General Edward Braddock was commissioned the first overall commander of military forces in British North America. The creation of a commander-in-chief for the American empire was only one of the many changes in imperial relationships occasioned by the last of the intercolonial wars. The increasing emphasis that the war focused on the colonies exposed American problems and situations to many of the English. Conversely, the presence of British military units in large numbers provided opportunities for colonists to view at close range the inner workings of the British army. Imperial relationships would never be the same after the war ended, for Britain and America now knew each other much more intimately than they had at any earlier time. And out of those circumstances would come motivations for imperial change.

In addition to military issues during the conflict, questions were generated about colonial commerce with enemy Caribbean islands and Britain's attempts to halt that trade, leading to suggestions for revising basic imperial structures that dated back to the Cromwellian years. Indian policy, land policy, ecclesiastical affairs, as well as such cost-accounting elements as revenue receipts and future military expenditures would provide the ingredients for fashioning new and radically different policies in the postwar "reconstruction" of the empire. The story of those changes, and the colonists' reactions to them, is another story—that of the coming of the American Revolution.

A SUMMING UP

By 1763 the British Empire was at least a century old. Created in the middle years of the seventeenth century, it was the offspring of mixed parentage, conceived to meet demands and desires of a rising group of English merchants, a revenue-seeking Crown, a landed gentry interested in increasing its income from the New World, and a group of committed "imperialists" who saw the nation's interests furthered by expansion of overseas enterprises. There had always been two empires. There was the theoretical empire, existing in the minds of some English statesmen and politicians, as well as in the minds of some American colonists— an empire in which the center (that is, the homeland) arranged the constitutional, political, economic, strategic, and other affairs for the imperial world. But there was another empire— the real, working empire that compromises, inefficiency, inattention, and ignorance had allowed to develop, and within which the American colonists played a more dynamic, more substantial role in policymaking. How separate and distinct those two empires had become began to be revealed in the last years of the old colonial system.

Economically, the empire had been a success. British commerce and industry had grown, and colonial commerce, and some colonial industries, had kept pace. The jealousies and fears of the rest of Europe directed toward Britain in the eighteenth century were proof of the success of the economic empire. Historians now seem generally agreed that, with a few significant exceptions, the American colonies also prospered economically under the old colonial system.

Britain allowed opportunities for political development in the colonies, although much of what took place occurred in spite of, not because of, imperial policies. The basic decisions and assumptions concerning local participation in political affairs, so different from the structure of New Spain or New France, permitted the rise of representative assemblies, the agencies that were to become the most distinctive and, in many ways, the most important political institutions in the American colonies. But other historical developments, as in the authorities of the royal governors, also modified the theoretical nature of imperial relationships and afforded opportunities for self-expression by the American colonists.

The British Empire at times was wracked with problems common to all "federal" organizations; centralizing and decentralizing forces collided to produce frictions. Whether such moments should be considered "normal" and a state of "perpetual discordance" the true tenor of the empire, or whether the collisions and frictions were minor set against the more imposing theme of harmony within the empire, historians do not, and perhaps never will, agree. But unquestionably the situations were complicated by the fact that time did not stand still. Colonial society underwent constant change, with accompanying stresses, during the century of imperial rule. With clashes between competing interests in the colonies occurring, it was perhaps inevitable that some groups would shape their policies to encompass cooperation with imperial agencies while others would use anti-imperial sentiments to enhance their local following.

Out of the varied experiences of those years, the American people gained the heritage that would define their nation in the decades and centuries to follow. The British Empire had offered them priceless opportunities to learn the art of self-government, to cultivate in a relatively unrestricted way social controls and economic opportunities more relaxed than had been known in the past. Easy acquisition of land, relatively free immigration, religious toleration created by necessity if not conviction, a fluid social structure in which individual attainment (ordinarily economic) rather than bloodlines counted—these were the distinctive features of the American colonial society. They would also become distinctive characteristics of the American nation.

Bibliographical Essay

The literature describing the relationships between the American colonies and the British Empire is voluminous, with the more general evaluations in older works; recent assessments tend to be fragmentary in nature, devoted to analysis of particular aspects of those relationships. Perhaps the most useful introductory statements are to be found in the appropriate textbooks in American colonial history. Of these, Clarence Ver Steeg's *The Formative Years, 1607–1763* (New York, 1964), deserves first mention, because within a relatively brief book Ver Steeg presents both current interpretations on a variety of topics and his own evaluations on others. His book contains a bibliographical essay with excellent annotations. This may be supplemented with Joseph E. Illick's bibliographical essay, "Recent Scholarship Concerning Anglo-American Relations,

1675–1775," in *Anglo-American Political Relations, 1675–1775*, Alison Gilbert Olson and Richard Maxwell Brown, eds. (New Brunswick, N.J., 1970), pp. 185–212. David Hawke's *The Colonial Experience* (Indianapolis, 1966) is a detailed statement of colonial history, with some of the virtues of Ver Steeg's book. A third general text is Max Savelle and Darold D. Wax, *A History of Colonial America*, 3d ed. (Hinsdale, Ill., 1973).

Moving from general textbooks to scholarly statements based on research in primary sources, Klaus E. Knorr, *British Colonial Theories, 1570–1850* (Toronto, 1944), provides a detailed introduction to the thoughts and interests responsible for the creation of the first British Empire. From there it is a natural step to the classical statements of the early twentieth-century "imperial" historians whose major works still constitute the most detailed, general accounts of imperial relationships. Charles M. Andrews's great work, *The Colonial Period of American History*, 4 vols. (New Haven, 1934–1937),* ranks first, with particular attention directed to the fourth volume entitled *England's Commercial and Colonial Policy*. The works of Herbert L. Osgood, *The American Colonies in the Seventeenth Century*, 3 vols. (New York, 1904–1907) and *The American Colonies in the Eighteenth Century*, 4 vols. (New York, 1924), might be consulted on specific questions. The third member, with Andrews and Osgood, of the founding triumvirate of the "imperial school," George L. Beer, presented his findings in *The Origins of the British Colonial System, 1578–1660* (New York, 1908); *The Old Colonial System*, 2 vols. (New York, 1912); and *British Colonial Policy, 1754–1765* (New York, 1907).

The "imperialists'" sympathy with Britain in her problems, and their tendency to ignore or de-emphasize internal colonial problems, led to modern reappraisals of colonial-imperial relationships. Many of these have been restricted to examination of specific aspects of, or episodes concerning, imperial affairs. Exceptions are the appropriate chapters of the well-balanced survey of *The Southern Colonies in the Seventeenth Century* by Wesley Frank Craven, the first volume in "The History of the

---

* Titles marked with an asterisk (*) are available in paperback editions.

South" series (Baton Rouge, La., 1949), and more recently in Craven's *The Colonies in Transition, 1660–1713* (New York, 1968).* An important contribution to understanding the first British Empire is Michael Kammen, *Empire and Interest: The American Colonies and the Politics of Mercantilism* (Philadelphia, 1970),* which provides a road map through the shifts in private and public groupings, from 1660 to 1783, in Britain and in America, that were the originators, beneficiaries, or victims of imperial politics and policies.

David S. Lovejoy, *The Glorious Revolution in America* (New York, 1972),* explores the early decades of the empire in the years from the Restoration to the 1690s. Lovejoy is particularly concerned with the colonists' perception of their rights in an age of increasing imperial control. The events of 1688–1689 are illustrated in the documentary collection *The Glorious Revolution in America* (Chapel Hill, N.C., 1964),* edited by Michael G. Hall, Lawrence H. Leder, and Michael G. Kammen. Leder has added further appraisals in *Robert L. Livingston and the Politics of Colonial New York, 1654–1728* (Chapel Hill, N.C., 1961), a fine case study of provincial politics and imperial relationships. Two additional studies balance imperial and colonial affairs in a judicious manner: Bernard Bailyn, *The New England Merchants in the Seventeenth Century* (Cambridge, Mass., 1955),* and Michael G. Hall, *Edward Randolph and the American Colonies* (Chapel Hill, N.C., 1960).* On Bacon's Rebellion, see Wilcomb E. Washburn, *The Governor and the Rebel* (Chapel Hill, N.C., 1957), and, for comparison, Thomas J. Wertenbaker, *Torchbearer of the Revolution* (Princeton, 1940).

As suggested in the second chapter of this book, a reader searching for evaluations of the economic aspects of the empire might begin with Oliver M. Dickerson's *The Navigation Acts and the American Revolution* (Philadelphia, 1951).* Although Dickerson is concerned with the pre-Revolutionary years, the first half of his book assesses the effects of the mercantile system on colonial economic development. Dickerson's assertions of beneficial effects from the imperial connection are too unqualified to satisfy some scholars, and the reader might balance Dickerson's views by examining Lawrence A. Harper, *The English Naviga-*

tion Laws (New York, 1939), and an essay by Harper, "The Effect of the Navigation Acts on the Thirteen Colonies," in *The Era of the American Revolution*, Richard B. Morris, ed. (New York, 1939).* Besides Harper's studies, additional qualifications may be found in Curtis P. Nettels, "British Mercantilism and the Economic Development of the Thirteen Colonies," *The Journal of Economic History* 12 (Spring 1952): 105–141. The same author's classic study of the interrelationships between currency and commerce is *The Money Supply in the American Colonies before 1720* (Madison, Wis., 1934).

More specific attention is devoted to particular aspects of economic regulation in Gilman M. Ostrander, "The Colonial Molasses Trade," *Agricultural History* 30 (April 1956): 77–84; the first part of Victor S. Clark, *History of Manufacturers in the United States*, rev. ed., 3 vols. (New York, 1929); in Arthur C. Bining, *British Regulation of the Colonial Iron Industry* (Philadelphia, 1933); and in Joseph J. Malone, *Pine Trees and Politics: The Naval Stores and Forest Policy in Colonial New England* (Seattle, 1965). Analyses of the mercantile empire derived from quantification of data (the product of "cliometricians") are illustrated in James F. Shepherd and Gary M. Walton, *Shipping, Maritime Trade, and the Economic Development of Colonial North America* (Cambridge, England, 1972). Stuart Bruchey has included documents relative to imperial regulation in *The Colonial Merchant: Sources and Readings* (New York, 1966).*

A fine introduction to the constitutional and political aspects of colonial-imperial relationships is Leonard W. Labaree, *Royal Government in America: A Study of the British Colonial System before 1783* (New Haven, 1930). Labaree's work will probably prove more useful than the generally noninterpretive volume by Arthur B. Keith, *Constitutional History of the First British Empire* (London, 1930). Specific studies of agencies of imperial control are numerous, but not all include analyses of the effects of regulation on the colonies. Among those that do are the older study of Oliver M. Dickerson, *American Colonial Government* (Cleveland, 1912), which concerns the Board of Trade, and the newer analysis of the connections between domestic politics and imperial policy by I. K. Steele, *Politics of*

Colonial Policy: The Board of Trade in Colonial Administration, 1696–1720 (Oxford, Eng., 1968). See also Dora M. Clark, *The Rise of the British Treasury* (New Haven, 1960); Thomas C. Barrow, *Trade and Empire: The British Customs Service in Colonial America* (Cambridge, Mass., 1967); and Carl Ubbelohde, *The Vice-Admiralty Courts and the American Revolution* (Chapel Hill, N.C., 1960).

In the last decade, historians have explored new dimensions of imperial arrangements as they sought understanding of the connections between British domestic and imperial politics. Representative essays are included in the above-cited Olson and Brown, eds., *Anglo-American Political Relations*; see also James A. Henretta, *"Salutary Neglect": Colonial Administration under the Duke of Newcastle* (Princeton, 1972); Stanley N. Katz, *Newcastle's New York: Anglo-American Politics, 1732–1753* (Cambridge, Mass., 1968); and Alison Gilbert Olson, *Anglo-American Politics, 1660–1775: The Relationship between Parties in England and Colonial America* (New York, 1973). Bernard Bailyn's *Origins of American Politics* (New York, 1968) views the royal governors' loss of real power, despite inflated theoretical authorities, as particularly responsible for "chaotic factionalism" as a hallmark of provincial politics.

There is no modern, general account of the office of royal governor, but the careers of individual governors have been detailed by John A. Schutz in *William Shirley: King's Governor of Massachusetts* (Chapel Hill, N.C., 1961) and in *Thomas Pownall: British Defender of American Liberty* (Glendale, Calif., 1951). Additional assessments of the office are contained in William W. Abbot, *The Royal Governors of Georgia, 1754–1775* (Chapel Hill, N.C., 1959). Jack P. Greene, in *The Quest for Power: The Lower Houses of Assembly in the Southern Royal Colonies, 1689–1776* (Chapel Hill, N.C., 1963),* delineates with care the various aspects of the elected assemblies' rise in real power during the eighteenth century.

Some of the works already mentioned contain evaluations of colonial political practices, but the "case" for a democratic colonial structure is best articulated by Robert E. Brown in *Middle-Class Democracy and the Revolution in Massachusetts,*

1691–1780 (Ithaca, N.Y., 1955), and Robert E. Brown and B. Katherine Brown, *Virginia, 1705–1786: Democracy or Aristocracy?* (East Lansing, Mich., 1964). Among the writings of those who view colonial society as less democratic, Merrill Jensen's essay, "Democracy and the American Revolution," *Huntington Library Quarterly* 20 (August 1957): 321–41, is representative.

The military and strategic aspects of the imperial connection may be studied in a variety of works. Howard H. Peckham, *The Colonial Wars, 1689–1762* (Chicago, 1964),* furnishes essential data; Douglas E. Leach, *Arms for Empire: A Military History of the British Colonies in North America, 1607–1763* (New York, 1973), is a fuller account. They might be used in conjunction with the first chapter of John Shy, *Toward Lexington: The Role of the British Army in the Coming of the Revolution* (Princeton, 1965),* in which the author discusses both imperial theory and practice in military matters. A specific study, detailing some aspects of interrelationships between colonies and empire during Queen Anne's War, is George M. Waller, *Samuel Vetch: Colonial Enterpriser* (Chapel Hill, N.C., 1960). Harry M. Ward, *"Unite or Die": Inter-colony Relations 1690–1763* (Port Washington, N.Y., 1971), examines military, Indian, and boundary problems, and traces British-colony relationships as well as those between separate provinces.

The Americans' response to imperial warfare is analyzed in the concluding part ("Warfare and Diplomacy") of Daniel J. Boorstin's *The Americans: The Colonial Experience* (New York, 1958),* a provocative volume which contains, in its earlier sections, analyses of other aspects of colonial society. Boorstin's description of colonial military affairs is quite different from the assessments of others, who see the Americans as aggressive and expansionistic. This view is reflected in Max Savelle, "The American Balance of Power and European Diplomacy, 1713–1778" in the above-cited Morris, ed., *The Era of the American Revolution.** (In the same volume, see Clarence E. Carter, "The Office of Commander in Chief: A Phase of Imperial Unity on the Eve of the Revolution.") Savelle's essay, and his book, *The Origins of American Diplomacy: The International History of Anglo-America, 1492–1763* (New York, 1967), place imperial-colonial situations within the framework of European diplomatic developments.

Relations between individual colonies and the mother country have been investigated in detail by Winfred R. Root in *The Relations of Pennsylvania with the British Government, 1696–1765* (Philadelphia, 1912) and by Trevor R. Reese in *Colonial Georgia: A Study of British Imperial Policy in the Eighteenth Century* (Athens, Ga., 1963). As Clarence Ver Steeg has noted, we need similar studies of other colonies.

The reader desiring source materials, in addition to the works of historians, will want to examine *American Colonial Documents to 1776*, edited by Merrill Jensen. This carefully selected volume of documents, complete with introductions and bibliographical notations, is Volume 9 of the Oxford University Press series, "English Historical Documents," David D. Douglas, gen. ed. (London, 1953–). Two briefer documentary collections are Joseph E. Illick, ed., *America & England, 1558–1776* (New York, 1970), and Jack P. Greene, ed., *Great Britain and the American Colonies, 1606–1763* (New York, 1970).

Finally, transcending in scope any of the categories indicated above, but helpful in understanding the history of any of them as related to the years from 1750 until the close of the colonial era, is the unique work by Lawrence H. Gipson under the general title, *The British Empire before the American Revolution*, 15 vols. (New York, 1936–1970). In those volumes may be found the most remarkable achievement of a single historian of American colonial history.

INDEX